Divorce?

You've Got This, Ladies!

It's Time to Live Your Best Life

BETH A. NOCAR

Biography

Beth A. Nocar, RN, MS, CCRN is a divorced mother of three who was born and raised in Baltimore, Maryland and currently resides in Stevensville, Maryland. Beth is a Critical Care Transport Nurse who received her undergraduate Nursing degree from Towson State University and her Master's degree in Trauma and Critical Care Nursing from the University of Maryland. With over 30 years of nursing experience working at the University of Maryland Medical Center in downtown Baltimore, Beth has witnessed both the fragility of life as well as the amazing strength of the human spirit. Beth's compassion to care, heal, and comfort have given her a unique ability to connect and communicate with people.

After her 19-year marriage ended as a result of her husband's adulterous affair, she found herself in need of the compassion and care of others. Her journey was one of struggle and triumph and true to her nature, she wanted to pay it forward with this book. Her hope is to help other amazing women navigate this incredibly difficult time and inspire them to live their best life.

When she isn't working or writing, you might find Beth having cocktails at the local dock bars, sunning herself on the beach, scuba diving exotic locations or off-shore fishing the Atlantic Ocean for yellow-fin tuna, mahi, or the elusive white marlin.

For Emily, David, and Anna

You lived it and you still love me.
And for that, I will be forever grateful.
I love you all, most ever!

TABLE OF CONTENTS

Preface

After almost 20 years of being married, imagine having life as you know it ripped out from under you. Imagine everything coming to a standstill. And to make matters worse, it was an affair with a friend of yours! The emotions swirl, endless: anger, bitterness, betrayal, confusion, helplessness, fear, sadness, and the list just goes on. "How am I going to get through this?" "What about the kids?" "What about our families and our friends?" "How do I get a lawyer?" "I can't imagine dating again." "I CAN'T DO THIS!" Well, my answer is, "YES YOU CAN!!!" You are stronger than you think! And, it is in these moments when you are down and out that you realize your true potential.

A critical care nurse by profession, this is exactly what I faced eight years ago, when I was 45 and had three children who were aged 16, 13, and 11. I believed I was married to my soul mate—someone I trusted with my life. We grew together from meager means and built a beautiful life for ourselves. He was there through my nursing and master's degree; we later married, purchased a home, had three children together, raised them up, and in between, my husband started his own company. There were wonderful vacations, a vacation home, and all the ups and downs that come along with being married to the love of your life. We had it all and we did it all as a team. We both had parents who were married for over 50 years. Marriages are never perfect, and there is always a certain degree of compromise involved, but I never imagined infidelity. All I imagined was growing old together. Well, guess who couldn't have been more wrong about it? Yep, it was ME!

Two years prior to the infidelity, a girlfriend of mine and I brought a single mom into our social circle. She had a daughter who was very good friends with our daughters. She was included in our intimate gatherings and planned social events, including football and Christmas parties. My friend watched her kids after school until she got home from work. I would run her kids to summer camp with mine after working the night shift. There were many sleepovers. Life was very busy—to say the least. I worked 12-hour-shifts in the night so that I was available for most of the kids' school events and activities—as my husband was busy building a successful company. I have no idea what transpired, and when, over the course of those last two years of marriage, but in the end, I found myself being left by my husband for this woman. Imagine someone who became your friend, saw your beautiful family, and was absolutely okay destroying it. I don't know about you, but in my world, women don't disrespect other women this way. Equally at fault was my husband. Adultery? How could he do that to me without even once telling me he was unhappy? How could he not want to fight for the love that we had? How was it so easy for him to walk out with zero remorse? He was a father. How could he hurt his children this way without flinching? The word devastating doesn't even begin to cover it.

For months, I was functioning in a fog, trying to get through each day, hour by hour and sometimes minute by minute watching the weight melt from my body uncontrollably. I just kept telling myself that I couldn't give up; my kids needed me. I needed to be strong for them. The result of my inspiring journey over the last eight years is this. It led me to write this book. My life as a nurse has been about helping people. It has been about healing, caring, coping, showing compassion, and being supportive in someone's hour of death. My work experience and life has brought me to such a positive place of strength and living that I felt the need to share my story in an attempt to help others through this amazingly difficult time.

Most of the few books that I found on this topic were either too technical, too long, or seemed incomplete. What I needed in my time of devastation was a quick read that was simple and to the point. I didn't want to be bogged down with unnecessary research, step by step approaches, or endless stories.

Some books focused too much on why he left instead of getting right to the pertinent information of how to begin healing. Most of them didn't mention how to deal with the legal process and more importantly, how to help your children. There were also many websites and blogs that I visited but found them to be too cumbersome and time-consuming. Technology at my age is a bit of a challenge. I still enjoy a good book in my hand.

I wish I had had this book during my initial hours of devastation, during my dark times along the way, and on days when I was making it a priority to live my life once again. Whether it was dealing with the anger and bitterness or my comical escapades of dating again, I just needed someone to tell me what to do. I just needed guidance when I was struggling. I was lucky enough to have an amazing group of friends and a supportive family, some of whom had been through a divorce themselves. I learned so much from each and every one of them and much of the wisdom they imparted to me is a part of this book.

Mid-life divorce after being married for many years brings with it a lot more baggage than you can imagine. And if you are reading this book, you know what I mean! It is important to know that it is a process. Not a clearly defined process because the experience is different for everyone, but there are many things that I found to be extremely profound and useful along the way that I know will help with your journey after the loss of your marriage. This is definitely a book for women. I've intended it to be a practical guide as well as a quick read with clearly defined chapters making it easy to find exactly what you are looking for depending on where you are in the process of your divorce journey. There is quite a bit of positivity, frankness, and even a little bit of humor in these upcoming pages. Just understand that it is one person's journey and one person's perspective. I can only hope that my journey is helpful in some way for your healing during what is arguably the most difficult time in your adult life. I hope it both inspires and empowers you to embrace your life that is still left to be lived and create a beautiful, new, and exciting next chapter of your own.

Introduction

I was dazed and confused as he walked out the door whistling a happy tune. My life as I knew it was totally blown out of the water and he was whistling? There was no remorse or empathy, at all. He was just suddenly gone. Infidelity was an absolute deal-breaker. I couldn't even process the emotions, let alone go to work, take care of the kids, or figure out how to get a divorce. I knew I needed help, and I needed it fast.

As a critical care nurse for over 30 years with a Master of Science Degree in Trauma and Critical Care, I have seen a lot in my profession and adapted quickly to the many changes, both good and bad. I have found myself in many situations where quick action was required to save the lives of my patients. I have dealt with a multitude of unexpected patient occurrences with competence and efficiency. The ending of my fairytale life with the man that I loved with all of my heart was an unexpected event, and I found myself having no quick action or competence to employ. And it burned.

During catastrophic events, your entire life tends to flash before you. And that is what was happening to me at that moment. I saw the girl who was the middle child of parents who were married for 50 years. My middle class, catholic upbringing with two hard-working parents who paid for three children to complete 12 years of school and four years of college flashed before my eyes. I worked three jobs at a time during my adolescence to not only save money but to pay for things that I wanted. I got my nursing degree and met the man who was to be my one and only. It was a life that went according to plan: my job as a nurse, living together, a master's degree, marriage, a new home, three children, my husband beginning a business, vacations, endless activities with the kids, a vacation home, and a boat. Both of us worked together as a team. We built an amazing life together. We supported each other in tough times and celebrated together during the good ones—the real American Dream. Too good to be true, eh? In my case, yep. There it was—an adulterous affair staring at me, right in the face. It was an unwelcome turning point forced upon me but a turning point nonetheless. Again, I needed help, and I needed it fast.

If you are reading this book, you too are experiencing similar anxieties and I'm so sorry for that. Just know that it is not your fault. Do not blame yourself for his decision and his behavior. He will more than likely try to place the onus on you because he is too much of a coward to accept responsibility for his actions but DO NOT buy what he is selling. He made the choices, not you.

I hope this book will be your lifeline for the help you need now and in the future. I will share insights into life immediately after the breakup and the importance of your mental health. The legalities of divorce can be quite overwhelming, time-intensive, and expensive. I will offer advice in this area that will be useful in your journey. I discuss several coping strategies in this book that you may want to try, hopefully embracing those that work for you. There will be some ongoing battles that I will cover which might force you to make some serious decisions for yourself. Kids also play a major role and you have to be on your A-game to ensure that they transition positively into this new life while minimizing the fact that they are in the middle of the messy divorce, too. You will need to move through the process of dealing with your emotions and deciding when you are ready to date and have sex again. It's definitely a road that takes careful navigation and it is not without roadblocks, cautions, and accidents. I will discuss my experiences and give positive advice in dealing with the pitfalls. Also included are a series of, what I will be referring to as, "profound moments," sprinkled throughout the book. They will serve as real game changers and result in more effective and positive paths.

To my dismay, many of these profound moments are what I wish I had known from day one instead of discovering them through my failures. Thankfully for you, you don't have to go through the same experiences. These revelations provided me with clarity, guidance, security, mental strength, and optimism. As a result, I was able to face my challenges with confidence and conviction. Although this doesn't happen overnight and is individual for everyone, this book is meant to inspire you to move forward and create your own happiness. Remember, anything is possible! Believe in yourself! I will empower and excite you for what comes next!

Chapter 1: My Profound Moments

L et's jump right in with my list of **Profound Moments**. These were revelations throughout my divorce journey that enabled me to conquer challenges by responding confidently in positive and effective ways. Some provided me with clarity and guidance, while others promoted mental strength and optimism. Although these are scattered throughout the book, I am adamant about providing information succinctly and quickly. After all, you need this information now and moving forward. These moments not only changed my perspective during my divorce journey but many of them, as I learned over time, would have been most beneficial since day one. I will discuss them more thoroughly as you read forward but I offer them to you now so you can start using them immediately. I want you to benefit from as many of them as possible from day one. These are uncharted waters for you. Since we all experience a somewhat different journey, keep in mind that you may discover some of your own profound moments along the way and that is great! The ultimate goal is a positive transition, and the more tools you get for navigation, the better.

Profound Moments

#1—If you were abandoned, you will probably never know the reasons why he left.

If I had known this early on, I might not have suffered so much wondering why or worse yet what I did. Let me make this clear: if you were left by your husband unexpectedly, this is not your fault. The thought that I might have done something wrong was all-consuming in the beginning and quite honestly a waste of my time. In the end, it doesn't matter. You still need to accept that your marriage is over and move forward. You had a life before you got married and you will have a great life afterward.

#2—For every 5 years of married life, you can expect 1 year of grieving.

This realization was provided by my counselor as I struggled with my frustrations of being unable to cope, in what I deemed to be, a timely manner. For me, I not only lost my husband but I also lost my best friend. Don't beat yourself up if you are struggling with the loss of your marriage and the life you used to know. It's similar to the loss of a loved one that you spent your whole life with. You never forget the memories, but it hurts you less as time passes by. Cut yourself some generous slack.

#3—The following books were life-changing:

1. *The Secret* by Rhonda Byrne

2. *Anger: Wisdom for Cooling the Flames* by Thich Nhat Hanh

These two books were extremely helpful and allowed me to move from a negative mindset to a positive one. I was amazed at how merely ridding my mind of the negativity brought positive things to me in every aspect of life. It was and still is pretty incredible. I can't wait for you to give it a try!

#4—Gratitude is important.

Tuning into what you can be grateful for will make you realize that how much you have is much greater and much more important than what you no longer have. It is definitely something that needs to be practiced regularly because the rewards for your psychological well-being are immense.

#5—Honesty is paramount throughout your journey, particularly during the legal process and with your children.

Nothing good comes from dishonesty. Lies breed more lies and then you get caught up in your own lies. Be truthful throughout all phases of the legal process. There is nothing more embarrassing and detrimental to your case than dishonesty. Just ask my ex-husband that. Being credible is essential if you intend to get what you want. As for your children, they need the security of a reliable parent during this time. Your honesty is essential in providing them with that stability.

#6—Choosing your lawyer is one of the most important decisions you will make.

Whether or not you have a lot of money, take time with this choice. The legal process is cumbersome and scary. You need someone you can trust and who is concerned about fighting for your best interest. For many, it is not only about competence but cost. Do your homework here to find your best fit. Don't forget to reach out to those that you know have already been through this. Their advice can be invaluable.

#7—Put your children at the TOP of your agenda.

Your children are your life. Just like you, they do not want to be in this situation. Keep them out of the middle. Don't use guilt or manipulation in your dealings with them. Your priority is to raise independent, responsible, and well-adjusted humans. Keep the grown-up stuff to the grown-ups. Put your children first in all situations.

#8—You are your child's parent, not their friend.

It is a guarantee that your children will use this opportunity to get what they want when they want it. They will even use guilt and manipulation to pit you and their father against each other. Don't fall for it. Maintain discipline and consistency.

#9—End the conflict between you and the father of your children.

This one is extremely tough but necessary. Continued conflict between you and your former husband hurts the children. They feel torn and unable to confide in either of you. Your kids will transition easier if you can be civil with each other.

#10—Take the higher road whenever possible.

This is a repetitive theme throughout the book. Your self-preservation and the well-being of your children depend on not engaging with negativity from your ex, no matter how tempting. Engaging in the ugly only results in hurt for you and for your children.

#11—Get a good handle on your anger and bitterness.

These emotions will be your biggest struggle from day one. I will discuss several coping strategies meant to ease the intensity of these feelings. Counseling may also be something you might want to consider. Your positive growth will depend upon conquering these emotions.

#12—Don't overthink things when it comes to dating and sex.

Yes, you will be doing this again someday. Yes, you might feel it's scary and unthinkable. Well, I'm here to tell you it wasn't as bad as I thought it to be. I think you will get a kick out of this part of my journey. I have survived and I am having great fun! And you will, too!

#13—Embrace your future!

Believe it or not, you will be doing this throughout your journey, even without knowing it. Each accomplishment will make you stronger and more empowered. You will take control. You will cope. You will be inspired. And you will live your best life! **You've got this!**

Chapter 2: Devasted, Down, but Not Out

The Dastardly Emotions

Okay ladies, let's make this chapter brief and stick to the point. After all, your goal is not to wallow and you want to get to the "How To" and not get stuck in grief. Yep, that was my philosophy. And now I say, "Good luck with that." You have just been crushed! YOUR MARRIAGE IS OVER! You are struggling with the WHY. And you have endless questions: "Why did this happen?" "How did this happen?" "What did I do wrong?" "What could I have done differently?" "How could he forget all the good times?" "How could he have no remorse?" "Why didn't he tell me he was unhappy?" "Why didn't he even try to make it work?" "How could he leave our kids?" "Why would he hurt them like this?" The questions swirl and swirl and swirl at random as you try to make sense of it. These questions and the corresponding emotions are all consuming, taking up every minute of every day, even keeping you up at night because you can't quiet your mind. Then, you begin with questions of the future. "How am I going to get through this?" "How will I stay strong enough for our children?" "How do I even go about getting a divorce?" Even the thought of dating again brings about a flurry of scary questions. "OMG, I now have to practice safe sex because I wasn't the one who was "fixed"!" "I'm going to have to worry about avoiding STDs? Are you kidding me? I am 45 years old! How is this fair? I did nothing wrong. I tried to be a good wife and a good mother and this is what I get?" All of it makes you sick to your stomach. At least, that is how I felt.

What you have just experienced is life-changing and whether you like it or not you need to face the emotions. You need to grieve. Being a nurse is all about being proactive with patient care. You need to be able to see things coming instead of reacting to them after your patient's condition has already deteriorated. So, in my case, I felt it necessary to be proactive with my grief. I wanted to get ahead of the game before the feelings got the best of me and I sought counseling. I know that counseling is not for everyone, but it was extremely beneficial to me. I made the decision for myself because I was extremely overwhelmed with many all-consuming emotions immediately after I was abandoned. There was shock, confusion, sadness, anger, bitterness, and fear. I couldn't eat. I couldn't sleep. Just about every minute of every day was consumed with thoughts of my happy marriage, thoughts of his betrayal, thoughts of how another woman who was my friend could betray me, thoughts of things I would miss, thoughts of the pain of our children, thoughts of the hurt of our family and friends, and thoughts of how I was going to face the future. The feelings definitely got the best of me and although I am not a depressed person, I felt as if I was becoming one. My fear of depression was real. I had my first counseling session within a month of his abandonment. I went once a week for several months. As my coping strategies improved, I was able to space my sessions further and further apart. I continued counseling for about two years throughout the divorce process. It was incredibly helpful in my healing. Counseling provided me **with Profound Moments #1** and **#2**. And let's be clear, I wasn't happy with **Profound Moments #1** and **#2**.

Profound Moment #1

Profound Moment #1 came when I was told by my counselor that I would probably never know the reasons why I was abandoned for another woman. I would probably never get the answers for all of my WHY questions, and my healing depended on me letting go of my inquiry. The answers would not take the hurt away or help me move forward. And she was correct. Instead, quite the opposite happened whenever I received any answers to the questions that I posed to my ex. He told the children and me that he didn't love me for the last ten years of our marriage. Now I knew that wasn't true because of some of the incredible experiences and successes we had had during those years, but nonetheless, it was a painful statement to process. He told me he wasn't leaving the kids; he was just leaving me and they would be fine— another lie. I cried and told him that I wasn't "fixed" because he was the one who had the vasectomy, and now I needed to worry about birth control in the future when I was ready to date again. I was told that it wasn't his problem anymore. Every answer I got was another stab in the heart. Then, you get answers that blame you for being the reason he left or cheated. He couldn't possibly take responsibility for having an affair and turning our lives upside down. In his eyes, it had to be my fault. That was the only way he could justify his behavior. I was loyal and loving, and that was supposed to be my fault? My point here is that this was my first game-changer. I was never going to get the answers I needed from him or more specifically he would never say what I wanted to hear. I was never going to get an apology for the hurt he caused me. I was just getting more and more hurt by being caught up in it.

Profound Moment #2

Profound Moment #2 occurred very early as well when my counselor said, "Beth, for every five years of marriage you can expect a year of grieving." To which I responded, "ARE YOU KIDDING ME?! I've been married for 20 years! I can't be like this for four years! I need to be functional for my kids!" At present, eight years into finding out about the affair, that timeline, for me, was very accurate. Even though I didn't want to hear this, it really was a game-changer for me. It gave me a time frame. I was certainly hoping to move through quicker than four years, but at least I knew that I wasn't a wallowing loser if it took me four years to get my act together. Everyone, annoyingly so, will tell you, "time heals." It's really the last thing you want to hear when you're shocked, angry, bitter, and depressed. You know everyone means well, but you just want to scream every time you hear it. I am here to tell you that you have to be patient with yourself. You cannot allow yourself to deny the feelings in the hope that they will go away. They won't go away. You need to allow yourself to feel it all—the sadness and tears, the anger and fears. Don't get discouraged if you bounce back and forth with your emotions. Believe me, just when you feel that your anger is diminishing, you may run into an old friend that triggers a memory of your ex and the emotions come flooding back again. It will be like a roller-coaster ride, only not as much fun. One day you might feel numb, not knowing how to get through your day of work, the next day you might be full of rage that could, unfortunately, spill over to your kids, coworkers, or friends. Then you have the "what if" days or the "I just want to stay in bed days." Have faith in yourself and your strength. Don't beat yourself up. Regain your clarity; apologize to those you hurt when you were angry. Look forward and not back, and get up and make that bed and admire how beautiful it looks and how great it is to only have to make one side of it instead of the whole thing! Begrudgingly, I'm going to say it, time really does heal. It takes much longer than you think it will to cope with the loss of your partner, the loss of your sense of family, and the loss of your dream of living happily ever after, but you will cope and you will heal.

Having an unbiased professional with experience to talk to was comforting for me. The realizations that I needed to be okay with not knowing why he left and that I needed to be okay with my grieving were just the beginning of my journey toward moving forward. It was progress. I felt rescued somehow. I finally had hope that the drowning would stop. It was the first bit of peace that I had felt since being pushed overboard. Counseling was also very beneficial in helping me to effectively deal with my emotions of anger and bitterness. This, in turn, allowed me to effectively deal and intervene with the emotions of my children as well as help them to positively cope and transition throughout the divorce process. Moving forward was always the goal, and counseling definitely enabled me to accomplish that objective.

I'm Drowning and I Need Help

It is important to realize that you can't do this alone. This is not a sign of weakness but one of strength. You have a desire to feel better and positively transform, and that can only come from a place of strength. Getting or asking for help is you pulling from the depths of that strength. Never be too proud to ask for help, and doing it alone just sucks anyway. Whether you choose to speak to a professional, a family member or a friend, vocalizing your emotions is cathartic, healing, and empowering. In my case, I chose all three and then some. I am that TMI (too much information) person. I know, ugh! I needed everyone in my boat to hear my play by play accounts of the day. For me, it was incredibly therapeutic! If I was going to stay afloat I needed to haul my parents, my siblings, my closest girlfriends, my coworkers, my counselor, and then eventually my lawyer, my financial advisor, and my accountant into the boat. Crazy right? I was extremely lucky to have such an amazing support system.

Danger! Danger! I have a word of caution here. Be careful not to overwhelm the people you choose to share your emotions with. There will be some who will tire of your tales of woe. Your goal is to keep supporters at this time, not chase them away. That's where I found a professional and those family members and friends who were divorced to be the most helpful. First, it's the professional's job to listen and those who had already experienced divorce were eager to impart their wisdom.

Within the first week, when I was lost, numb, and moving through each day in a fog, two of my divorced girlfriends told me to bring paper and a pen, and they were armed with wine. These two were and still are amazing women. They were my neighbors at the time, both with similar stories to my own and I am still very close to them to this day. Ironically enough, we all lived on the same side of our cul-de-sac. We still joke about how our side of the street was cursed, particularly since our zip code ended with the numbers 666. By the end of that evening, not only was I happily buzzed and actually smiling, I left from there with a pad full of information for my lawyer. They spent the evening making me write down everything I needed to ask for, everything I was going to need to be aware of, and everything I should expect through the legal process. I even left with a list of lawyers and questions I needed to ask during my consultations. It was both marvelous and reassuring! It was a small step, but nonetheless, a step forward. With their assistance, I finally had a little bit of clarity in what seemed like a daunting situation.

During those initial weeks and months, you will need as much support as you can get to maintain whatever sanity you have left after being dealt your horrific blow. The upcoming pages of this book can be your guide to navigating your emotions, your children, and the legal processes. At this early juncture, you will need to get an immediate handle on your emotions in order to discover and incorporate appropriate coping strategies that you can utilize to progress in a positive way. I will tell you how. This will then allow you to deal more effectively with the emotions and coping of your children. Your children need to be your priority from day one, and I cannot emphasize that enough. Their future as responsible and well-adjusted human beings depends on a positive transition during this difficult time. I will tell you how. The legalities surrounding divorce and child custody are overwhelming and intimidating. I will tell you what to expect and how to prepare. Remember: You are beautiful! You are strong! **You've got this!**

Chapter 3: Chin Up! You Are a Fighter

By now, you are aware of how oppressive your emotions have become. They are interfering with every facet of your life both day and night. Your kids are suffering, and you can barely help yourself—let alone help them and try to answer the multitude of questions. On top of that, you have to actually get the divorce and you have no clue how to go about it. All of this makes you feel like someone blew a hole in your stomach. The sickening feeling is real. The suffering has got to be dealt with. Hold your head high and strap on those boxing gloves because it's time to pull yourself together. You need to begin learning how to cope with all of this. Your functionality depends on it. As I discuss many of the things that helped me to survive my bout in the ring, it is my hope that some of these coping techniques will resonate with you. Incorporate as many as you can to ensure that you finish on top.

Self-Care

Taking care of yourself is paramount throughout your journey. It is important for both your coping and your healing. Eating and sleeping are key, but don't be discouraged if neither goes well for you in the beginning. Stress has a way of disrupting your sleep and appetite. For some, sleep is impossible because you can't seem to shut off your mind. It never seems to stop detailing the events, feeling the hurt, and almost imploding with unanswered questions. For others, you may want to stay in bed and never get out while still dealing with the same turmoil in your mind. This can sometimes spiral into a depression. In terms of appetite, you either overeat in times of stress or not at all, and I'm sure at this point, you know which category you fall into. Avoid the extremes when it comes to eating. Get up and out of that bed every day, jump in the shower, and eat.

Exercise of any kind is also good when it comes to taking care of yourself. It is not only good for your body but a good distraction for your mind. A word of caution for the minimal eaters in times of stress, exercising could cause further weight loss and send you into another spiral of health problems. I enjoyed exercise, but I also knew my weight was rapidly dropping because I wasn't eating much due to a lack of appetite. I had a wake-up call from a very funny and supportive male friend. I'm a believer that God puts people in your path for a reason. It happens time and time again for me. Anyway, I digress. My friend hadn't seen me in a while, and he was on the treadmill next to me and we were chatting. He said, "Girl you need to get yourself off this treadmill and go get yourself a burger!" We laughed, but it was at that moment that I was really able to see how I looked. It was at that point that I began forcing protein shakes, exercising for strength instead of calorie burning, and really exploring coping mechanisms that would work to get me to a healthy weight.

Yoga and meditation became very instrumental to me. Although not for everyone, I was so glad I tried both. I not only enjoyed them but I incorporated them into my life and continue doing both even today. I found the mind and body connection to be unbelievably healing. There are free apps out there for both meditation and yoga if you want to give it a try. It may just be what you need.

As women and mothers, many of us do everything for others and not for ourselves. How about a massage? A manicure and pedicure? A new hair color or hairstyle? A night out or a trip with girlfriends? Almost unheard of, am I correct? If you can afford it, now is your time to do it! It's time to look and feel good about yourself.

Self-care obviously means different things to different people. What matters to me may not matter to you. Only you can decide what will make you feel your best. I encourage you to try as many things as possible. For me, self-care is about taking care of myself mentally and physically. I enjoy going to the gym for spin cycling, yoga, and Pilates. My eating and sleeping corrected themselves over time. When I can't sleep because my mind is in overdrive, meditation works the best for me. I really enjoy meditation, and I am trying to get in the habit of making time for it in the morning. It does wonders to clear my mind before I start my day. I like guided meditation, so I use free apps on my phone. Even if I can only do it for five minutes, it's worth it. It took me a few years but now I try to get a massage and a mani/pedi once a month, and I get my hair done every eight weeks. I make time for my girlfriends and one-on-one time with my kids. What a difference all of it has made in how I feel about myself and how much better of a person I am to others.

I know you are overwhelmed right now, but be thankful for another day because this, too, shall pass. You have too much to live for. Even if day by day seems too long then think hour by hour or even minute by minute, if necessary. You deserve caring, so do it for yourself!

Meds vs. No Meds

Do I need to be medicated to cope with this? This is a dilemma for some and a "no brainer" for others. I have no advice here other than to consult a medical expert if you feel that you need medication. There is absolutely no shame in taking meds to deal with the anxiety and depression that grief can cause. This is an individual decision based on your ability to cope during difficult times. Only you and your healthcare professional can determine this together. Separation and divorce are very stressful, particularly the first days, months, and possibly years. Some people gain weight, whereas I lost it. At 5'7 and about 135 pounds, I dropped to a scary 116 pounds. I was trying to drink protein shakes to gain weight to no avail. I did seek counseling for myself. I did not choose medication, although some people in my family felt that I should have. Again, please understand that it is not shameful to take medication to cope. Just because I didn't, doesn't mean you shouldn't. My counselor and I discussed my options and for me, consistent counseling was all I needed. There is no right or wrong here. The focus should be you being able to face and manage the barrage of emotions while effectively dealing with your children, your job, your health, and the divorce process. The worst thing you can do is ignore the emotions. It sucks but you need to live it and feel it in order for the healing process to begin. It is important to realize that seeking counseling and/or taking medication is not a weakness. In order for you to take care of your responsibilities and others, you must first take care of yourself. You need to do what is best for you.

Coping Aids

Along the way, I found so many things to be incredibly helpful to cope with the separation. However, what works for some may not for others. Some things cost money and others do not. Let me be clear, you do not have to have money to get through this. Sharing your feelings with your family and friends doesn't cost money. Prayer doesn't cost money. Listening to music doesn't cost money. Exercise doesn't cost money. Journaling and positive thinking don't cost money.

Your inner strength is what will get you through and WE ALL HAVE INNER STRENGTH. You may not feel strong right now but the human spirit is innately resilient. We have the ability to adapt and thrive. In fact, adaptability is common in most species. It's how we survive. Survival of the fittest, correct? You just need to dig deep and bring it to the surface. You have the power to overcome your circumstances. You need to believe in that and believe in yourself. There are many coping strategies and from my experience, I am certain that you will be able to find something that will work for you.

Family

Family can be tricky. Whether they are supportive or not may depend on their cultural or spiritual beliefs. Obviously, if they are not accepting of divorce, they will not be helpful. However, if they do love you, they will eventually come around (if they truly want to see you happy).

I am very lucky. I have an extremely supportive family. Although my parents have been married for over 55 years, both of my siblings had been through divorces but unlike mine, theirs were amicable. If anything, I was sad because I thought I had the marriage like my parents that would last until "death do us part." Nevertheless, my parents and my siblings were able to support me emotionally. There were phone calls to check up on me. There were conversations about what to expect regarding my emotions and the legal process. There were outings for meals and drinks to keep my spirits up. My sister was instrumental in helping me with my lawyer search. Thankfully, I didn't have to depend on them a great deal because I had so many amazing friends but they made it clear that they were there if I needed anything. They just wanted me healthy and happy, both emotionally and physically. I am forever grateful to have been blessed with such a supportive and loving family.

Friends

Friends played the most important role in my healing, and hopefully you are experiencing much of the same. Most of them want to be there for you and many of them have an intimate experience in what you are going through. Reach out to them, and listen to what they have to say. Take in what is useful and leave what is not. These folks will have a profound impact on how well you move forward by sharing not only their stories of hardship and divorce but their advice of how they got through. You will inevitably be left with the fact that, in some cases, others have been dealt a more severe blow.

As they share their life experiences, much of what they say will stick with you. I heard statements such as "time heals," "take the higher road," "don't put the kids in the middle," "you have to kiss a lot of toads before you meet your prince," and my all-time favorite, "karma's a bitch." Ladies, you will love that one! Bad Karma comes to those who have done you wrong. I promise! It may take years but it happens. And you will smile. There is also incredibly good Karma. The more you take the higher road, and I'm very well aware of how difficult it is, the more good will come to you. I've lived it, more than a few times, and it's astonishing.

Again, just a word of caution. be careful how much you rely on your friends.

Some can handle your constant "woe is me" and others cannot. From my experience, everyone is very supportive in the beginning when you are in crisis. Everyone wants to help. Months down the road, however, when it is still all-consuming for you, you will be able to identify those who can still handle your tales of frustration and those who just wish you would "move on already." I found that those who had been through a divorce were always willing to listen and continue to give advice. We all need friends. Be careful not to push anyone away.

I had a group of seven ladies who were always there for me in one way or another throughout my journey and still are. I had my loyal forever friend who I met in college and we have become like family. We are godmothers to each other's children, and she is referred to as aunt by my kids and I am aunt to hers. It is nice to have that friend who shows up no matter what, and she always shows up when I need her.

Another of my girlfriends would call me almost daily on her way to work or on her way home from her second job at night. She was my sounding board for the day's events, both positive and negative. She was such a supportive listener, and her empathy was my ray of sunshine when I got caught up in the rain of my negativity. She never failed to mention what a great person and mother I was. Her healing words inspired me to keep fighting for my happiness.

I have two other girlfriends who I refer to as the dynamic duo. We had met through our children. They were my village when it came to my children, particularly my son. They were and still are always up for a girls' night out. Both are married but have included me in everything, from family parties to family trips. So many great times and great memories were made and continue to be made. They helped me cope by keeping me distracted with fun, fun, and more fun!

I also have a girlfriend who was unlucky enough to be in the middle. Our daughters had been close friends since kindergarten and her husband was good friends with my former husband. She and I were the ones who brought my ex's paramour into our social circles. After I was abandoned, I'm sure it was very difficult for my girlfriend but she never hesitated to listen and empathize particularly with the drama surrounding texts with my ex. She was great at talking me down. She was also my friend who prepared meals for the kids and me. Those meals were Godsend when I was completely overwhelmed. She would also get me out on her boat with friends to keep me distracted in a positive way. Unfortunately for her, she has just recently gone through a divorce, but I am grateful that I could pay it forward to her throughout her divorce journey.

Then, of course, there were my two neighbors, both of whom were my divorced girlfriends. We met when they were all married. One lived next door to me and the other down the street. They were both there for each other during each of their divorces. Although I was there for them, it wasn't in any way close to how they were there for me. They were pivotal in jump-starting me on my legal endeavor to divorce. They knew the drill, and they weren't about to let me get screwed by my ex. They had me write lists of what I needed to ask for in terms of alimony, child support, and assets, just to name a few. And write it all down I did! I even had names of lawyers to consult with. This was so valuable in decreasing my anxiety toward the legalities of divorce. I didn't even know where to begin, and they solved that problem for me. The best advice that my neighbor down the street gave me was to try to plan trips every three or four months even if it was just a weekend with family or friends. She said it was important to have something to look forward to and distract me from the daily onslaught of negative emotions. She was so right! My next-door neighbor's marriage ended almost exactly like mine with her husband unexpectedly abandoning her for another woman. She was able to relate so completely with my emotions of anger, resentment, and broken heartedness. She was pretty much a daily walk for me, and I went to her house on most days to vent. I'm sure I was exhausting for her. After all, listening to me couldn't have been easy, having to relive her own nightmare. But she never stopped listening, consoling, and advising. Having gone through something similar, years before me, she was my role model. Her perspective from her experience was so helpful for me to overcome my emotions. I aspired to be in the positive place that she had created for herself. We would go on bike rides and travel together often. She inspired me to start journaling and to try yoga and meditation. She also suggested great books to me that had helped her through her dark times. Although these two awesome ladies no longer live on my street, they are still a huge part of my life. My next-door neighbor now lives in Cleveland, Ohio but we visit each other once or twice a year, and my other neighbor is happily remarried and they include me in just about everything they do from boat trips to local dock bars to gatherings with family and friends.

Having said all of this, it would be unfair if I didn't mention how much my co-workers were a part of my coping and healing. Work in itself was healing. Although difficult to turn off the emotions, the stresses of my job and the high acuity of my patients forced me to be laser-focused on them and their care. It was nice to be free of those constricting emotions during my 12-hour-shifts, especially around the meal table. I was always entertained, and the conversations usually got colorful and graphic. We shared many tears of laughter around that meal table together. The smiles were especially welcomed during my low points. In particular, I was lucky to work for about 25 years with a phenomenal paramedic and friend. She kept me sane and focused during our shifts together in those initial days, months and years after I was abandoned. She was my sounding board at work and she never tired of listening with an empathetic ear when I needed to voice my frustrations. Although we no longer work together, she still checks in on me or we go to dinner from time to time. She still tags me on social media when she finds inspirational or prophetic quotes and memes that remind her of me. It's crazy how they seem to pop up just when I need them.

I have no word other than "blessed" to describe all the friends that God has placed in my path along the way. They always came when I needed them the most. I'm sure you have friends that are already reaching out to you but if that is not the case, reach out to them. You will find that they are more than willing to listen and support you. They are invaluable coping tools.

Spiritual Support

My faith was a tremendous outlet for coping with the variety of issues brought on by divorce. This may not be for everyone based on individual beliefs, but for me, church services and prayer provided me with great emotional solace. Although both have been a consistent part of my routine throughout my entire life, they had a greater significance at that point. I would go to church, and the sermons seemed to be directed at what I was going through at that moment—as if God knew what message I needed that particular week; it seemed like He was speaking directly to me. It was uncanny, but it strengthened my beliefs. Prayer was paramount every night and sometimes throughout the day, if it was a particularly difficult one. Oftentimes, spiritual or religious organizations offer pastoral counseling, group meetings, and other resources for those going through a divorce. It might be beneficial to research what is available in your area or within your spiritual or religious group.

Travel

Traveling was another coping mechanism for me. As I've said before, one of my divorced girlfriends suggested that it was beneficial for her to take small trips every three or four months. She said it was helpful in putting her mind on to something other than the consumption of the divorce. She was absolutely right! Understand that this does not need to be expensive. It can be visiting a friend or family member for the weekend. The planning and the anticipation of something positive, as well as the trip itself, was a welcome distraction. I took my kids with me most of the time and that was great for their coping as well! I also did some travel on my own, which was extremely empowering!

I took my friend's advice a little over a month after my husband left. It was only a weekend at the beach with the kids and it was Mother's Day. Who knew it would be one of the best Mother's Day! It was so full of love and laughter. We rode bikes on the boardwalk, went to the beach, and played games. Life felt normal even if it was just for a weekend. Travel was a little difficult at first because I don't believe in my kids missing school, but we did make trips to the beach throughout that summer. By the fall, I took the kids to Disney World for an extended weekend when they were off from school. That winter, I took them to a fairly local, kid-friendly hotel with a pool just after the new year. It was a place they enjoyed growing up. For spring break, we went to Atlantis in the Bahamas. Over the years, we have had several trips together. Some were as small as weekends with friends at amusement parks or weekend college visits, and others were grander like our trips to Hawaii and Tahiti. Some of our vacations included traveling with other families to the beach for the 4th of July and to Aruba. We've skied the Colorado mountains of Vail and Lionshead. We made visits to New York and even took a coastal California road trip from San Francisco to San Diego. My kids still talk about many of these trips today. And what is most comforting is that their memories are not as much about what we did as about how they felt spending quality time together.

The travel I did by myself got more courageous over time. Initially, on my weekends without the kids, I would spend time with girlfriends just hanging out for drinks, dinner, or boat rides. My first real trip on my own was to Las Vegas with my former next-door neighbor. This was after my divorce was finalized, a year after being abandoned. Three years after the divorce, I actually went totally alone to a health and wellness spa. I was so profoundly affected in a positive way by that experience that I have since then visited it a few more times. You would be surprised by the wealth of health and wellness retreats that are out there just waiting for you. I have also been to Miami for a girl's weekend and have tagged along with them and their husbands to Nashville. I've even gone to London for an NFL football game. Now I travel to see my children, and they travel to see me.

I have to admit that traveling without my partner was surprisingly not difficult. I'm not really sure why. Maybe because he hurt me. Maybe because my friends were so inclusive. It was probably both. What was most difficult at first was being without my kids. I worried about them being okay without me. There was quite a bit of confusion, turmoil, frustration, and anger during their weekend visits with their father for at least the first two years after he left. They were a bit resentful when they knew I was going somewhere, and they had to be with their father. I felt guilty that they weren't with me. It was a big adjustment for me as well as for them. As they got older and could speak for themselves, I worried less. Over time, my guilt lessened because I also realized that I needed my time to recharge. Ultimately, I was a better parent because of it.

Again, traveling does not have to be an expensive and extravagant endeavor. It just needs to be about distraction and positive emotions. For me, some trips were for fun and those were mostly the ones that I took with my children. Other trips were definitely to unwind and recover, which were usually trips I took by myself. Soak in everything you can. Whether it's escaping to a destination or just somewhere local, get going! It's good for your soul.

Reading

Reading was also very good for me. I've always enjoyed reading, just never really had enough hours in the day while working and raising my children. This time in my life, it was different. I needed guidance and information. I read anything that was inspirational and fit the genre of self-help.

Profound Moment #3

My favorites were *The Secret* by Rhonda Byrne and *Anger: Wisdom for Cooling the Flames* by Thich Nhat Hanh. I would have to give this the **Profound Moment #3** designation. Both were surprisingly transformational for me. There were a few other Rhonda Byrne books that inspired me as well. Her Daily Teachings, which is a compilation of 365 daily insights, was not only thought-provoking but useful for me to heal and be in control of my best life. For those of you who feel that reading is a chore, I suggest short reads, something you can get through quickly. Choose books that share personal experiences. It's comforting to know that you are not alone and that others have been in positions similar to yours. Soak in as much as you can and don't forget to read for pleasure. Pleasure is uplifting during times of sadness. The distraction itself makes it worth it. Every moment spent on reading lessens your sorrows. Oh, and girl, the Fifty Shades series is not to be missed! There's no shame here. I read them cover to cover and have watched the movies several times. Read erotic romance novels. There is nothing wrong with fantasizing about how you would like your life to be. We may be middle-aged, but we are not dead! All jokes aside, don't give up on romance. You may be swearing off men right now. I certainly did. But trust me, you will be ready again. It may take months or years (as in my case) but you will be ready. Read about it, want it, and experience it! Let's face it, you may be down but you're not out! There's a whole other fun chapter about that coming up.

Music

Always a crowd-pleaser, music has traditionally captured every emotion and life event imaginable. Within weeks of being left, songs on the radio during my car rides began to resonate with me. Again, I had the feeling of Divine intervention, like I was meant to be hearing those songs in those exact moments. The minute a song spoke to me, I would add it to my phone. *Stronger* by Kelly Clarkson and *I Will Survive* by Gloria Gaynor were two such songs. They became the first songs on the very first playlist that I ever created on my phone. I named the playlist "My Inspiration." There were days when I was super low, and I would blare these songs and sing along to the top of my lungs. Sometimes I would even dance as well. It was the kind of music that had an inspiring message to keep me pressing on. I would even play these songs when I was getting ready to go out with my girlfriends. This playlist has expanded over the years and now includes songs such as *Broken and Beautiful* by Kelly Clarkson, *Marvin Gaye* by Charlie Puth, *Happy* by Pharrell Williams, and *Good as Hell* by Lizzo, just to name a few.

Make it a point to create playlists on your phone. I also had a "My Calm" playlist, which included music that would calm me when I was frustrated or angry. I needed those songs very early on as well. I guess you can call it my "count to ten music." It included *Don't Worry Be Happy* by Bobby

McFerrin, *One Moment in Time* by Whitney Houston, and *The Climb* by Miley Cyrus. It also included Contemporary Christian and Gospel music.

Music was always fun when it came to my kids as well. I can't tell you how many videos we have, at one time or another, with us singing in the car, in the house, and on trips. We shared many laughs and bonding moments with music. My kids even suggested new songs for my playlists.

Concerts are also fun. I've attended them with friends and some of them with my children. Music is empowering. Use it. As it did with me, it will pull you from the depths of despair, pull you from your anger, and inspire you to more positive places in your mind. You will be amazed to see your progress as you create more playlists. It will be a musical journal of your transformation!

Journaling

Journaling was another thing that I found to be extremely powerful. This was a suggestion from my next-door neighbor. She even bought me a beautiful journal, which is now already full and I am on to another one. Somehow getting it all out on paper was a release for me. It was also helpful for recalling events that would have otherwise been forgotten due to the confusing and foggy times during the initial trauma. Many times, writing diffused my anger. My journal was cleansing. I used it as a release of emotion, a wish list for what I wanted in my life, a clarification of who I was and who I wanted to be, a source from which I drew information for the legal process and a place to document gratitude.

Profound Moment #4

Gratitude is important and marks **Profound Moment #4**. Start by making a list of five to ten things that you are grateful for, especially during times when you are feeling low. When I first started my gratitude journal, I wrote ten things for 30 consecutive days to get me in the habit. I wrote what I was grateful for and why. For example, on Day 1, six out of the ten things I was grateful for were people. These were my kids, my parents, my in-laws, my siblings, and my friends. By Day 30, I was grateful for certain moments like spending time with my oldest daughter, a phone call from my mom, a weekend at the beach with my son, and being able to pay all of my bills. Remember, don't forget to include why you are grateful for each of the things that you have listed. It requires a bit more thought but intensifies the sentiments. The more grateful I was, the more favorable things kept happening in my life. You will be surprised at the positive effects it has on your outlook. After years, I have gone back and read my journal from the beginning and it is remarkable how far I have come. I saw that inner strength throughout the pages as well as my positive transformation. I still continue to journal to bask in the happiness of life and to carry on with the journey of gratitude. This one is free and comes highly recommended, ladies!

Power of Positive Thinking

This one may be tough, especially in the early phases of your separation and divorce. However, I want to tell you that the benefits are immediate. It is so easy to get caught up in negativity, both internal and external. It does nothing but continue your downward spiral. You have to break the cycle. Until you start to see the positive, the negative will continue to happen. The more you think you can't do it, the more it won't be done. The more you think you don't have money, the less money you will have. The more you think things will continue to go wrong for you, the more things will go wrong. The more you can replace a negative thought with a positive one or surround yourself with positive people instead of negative ones, the quicker you will notice your favorable evolution. Again, a concept that is hard to make sense of, but I assure you that it works, and it has worked countless times for me for sure.

Positive thinking takes some time to master, but consistent self-censorship is key. By this, I mean that you have to keep yourself in check at all times. You need to catch yourself in the negative thought and flip your mind to something positive. For example, using curse words is a problem for me. Most of the time, my cursing is not used in a negative way, and it's more for embellishment. I will use curse words in general conversation when I'm telling a funny story or just recounting the day's events. Sometimes, curse words just seem to make what is being said come alive, more relatable, and even humorous. According to my friends, I'm quite entertaining! Nonetheless, depending on whose presence you are in, it can be disrespectful. As a matter of fact, my dad is not a fan of hearing a certain foul word that begins with an F leaving my lips, and he never fails to reprimand me with his looks of disappointment. Just like giving up food for a diet, I have chosen many times to give up curse words. At first, it is difficult, but the more that I pay consistent attention to it and catch myself in the act, the easier it is to stop. The same goes for ridding yourself of negative thoughts. Once I read The Secret by Rhonda Byrne about six months into my struggle, I was on my way to mastering this concept. Give it a try! It's another free one!

Coping with the divorce process and your emotions at each phase is probably the most difficult and lasting part of the journey. The struggle is real and continues for me even years later. There is no avoiding future life events that will naturally stir up old wounds and feelings. Whether it's your kids' activities, graduations, weddings, funerals, or just running into your ex accidentally, you will need to dig deep and rely on one of the above coping mechanisms to get you through. It gets easier as time goes by. You are consumed by it less and less. It's satisfying when the time comes when he never enters your mind at all, unless triggered by an outside event. So, keep your chin up and be the fighter you know you are. You will not be knocked out. Remember you are a winner! **You've got this!**

Chapter 4: Bad Karma's a Bitch for Liars

At this point, let's do a self-check. So, you're still devastated and still going through all of the emotions I mentioned earlier but at least now you have a glimmer of hope for a positive recovery. You also realize that you will have to simultaneously tackle the legalities of getting a divorce. The thought actually makes you feel nauseous. This chapter is meant to ease your mind a bit and provide the clarity you will need to navigate the sometimes crazy seas.

The divorce process is, hands down, the worst part! It is overwhelming, cumbersome, and time-consuming. Although this information is dry and uninteresting, it will be essential for your future well-being. So, pay attention! The most important piece of advice that I can give here is HONESTY!

Profound Moment #5

Honesty is **Profound Moment #5**. Lies lead to more lies; then, not only can you not remember the lies you told, but you also get caught up in them. I'm not going to lie, no pun intended, it's extremely gratifying to watch your spouse get caught up in his own lies at court. The bad karma that it brings him is satisfying and laughable. Don't allow this to happen to you. Tell the truth. Be on the good side of karma.

When it comes to the legalities of divorce, the enormity of what you are feeling right now is undeniably staggering. Everyone who has gone through it was in your same boat. Refuse the urge to jump overboard. Instead, be the Captain of your vessel and take that job seriously! You do need to educate yourself. There are plenty of online resources to get you started and every state has different requirements. All states require a judge to review and approve the divorce. If spouses cannot agree on a settlement, the judge decides how property will be divided and how parenting time will be shared. You will need to investigate how long you must reside in your state before you can file for divorce, how long you must wait before your divorce can be finalized after you file it, and how your state treats child support and alimony.

If possible, at all, mutually agreeing on a settlement is, in most cases, more financially beneficial. Going to court gets expensive and ugly! Trust me, I know from experience. My ex and I were unable to reach an agreement. It went from exchanging what seemed like an immense amount of paperwork and information, to settlement negotiations, to mediation, to court hearings, and then, finally, our case was heard before a judge in court. It was ugly, both emotionally and financially. In my case, my ex had been planning his exit for months and I had no clue about it. He thought I wouldn't know or find out about all of our assets. He tried to rob me of what was rightfully mine after almost 20 years of marriage. Although I tried very hard to settle out of court multiple times, an agreement was never reached. And to make matters worse, my ex appealed the judge's decision. So, the decision that took almost two ugly years to get, took another three years after more information sharing, mediation, depositions and a hearing before the Court of Special Appeals— only for him to receive decisions, in all cases, that were worse than what I was willing to settle for! Again, "Karma's a Bitch." I tried my best to avoid court, and I was rewarded for trying to do the right thing and being honest. Although very expensive and emotionally and physically exhausting, what I stood to gain and what I rightfully deserved outweighed the expenses. The way I saw it, after dedicating my life to my family, I owed it to my children to ensure that I could take care of them financially as well as of myself and my future. The decision to settle or fight is purely an individual one. I have no regrets for my decisions, and I want no regrets for you. Your spouse will try to take advantage of your fragile emotional state. DO NOT LET THIS HAPPEN! Fortitude is the strongest word I can convey to you. You will need all of your strength and courage to successfully navigate your ship. You will be tested. You will be tempted to lie. You will have to compromise. You will have to take the higher road. This part of the journey will intensify your emotional roller-coaster. You need to put on your big girl panties and brace yourself for the storms ahead.

Lawyer

Your first step is to acquire legal counsel. You need to know your legal rights and responsibilities. This is probably the most important decision you will make.

Profound Moment #6

I repeat, choosing your lawyer is one of the most important decisions you will make and therefore it is **Profound Moment #6**! Do your research. Meet with several divorce lawyers and take a friend or family member who you can count on to take notes and evaluate with you. Your state of mind will, more than likely, be fragile at this point. You need someone by your side who can provide clarity. It is also helpful if this person has been through a divorce but this is not an absolute requirement. Some lawyers give free consultations, while others require a fee. This fee is usually applied to your bill if you decide to retain that particular lawyer. Keep in mind, once you consult with a lawyer, your husband cannot retain his/her services because of conflict of interest. Therefore, if you can afford to see several lawyers, especially if you think it's going to get ugly, see as many of the best lawyers that you can to limit your husband's choices. This will get expensive, so only do what you can afford. Your goal is to stay away from things getting ugly and save money at the same time.

I only visited two lawyers because at the time when I was embarking on my divorce, I didn't know all of this. One of the lawyers was local, and one was 20 minutes away. My sister was my person, and she accompanied me to both, which was extremely comforting. She had been through a divorce and was better prepared with questions and what to expect. She took notes on everything the lawyers said as I tearfully recounted my story. I answered what questions I could, and she asked questions that I was too distraught to remember or just didn't think about.

There are consultation fees and retainer fees. The consultation fees are paid to meet with the lawyer to see if he or she is the right fit for you and what you need. Some consultations, as I've said, are free. There are a lot of free legal services offered locally as well. Some of my divorced friends have used them. You just need to contact your local courthouse to inquire about what free services they have. The retainer fee is money paid upfront to secure the services of the lawyer. No legal work will be performed on your behalf until this retainer is paid. The lawyer will draw on this money as the case proceeds until it is exhausted; then you will be billed for services provided beyond that amount. This fee is based on the number of hours that the lawyer projects he or she will spend on your case. For example, if the attorney charges $100/hour. and plans to spend 10 hours on your case, he or she will charge you a $1,000 retainer fee.

The local lawyer I visited was a free consultation, and the other attorney I visited cost $900. He was an expensive consultation because those who knew about the conflict of interest would consult with him and not retain his services just so their husband or wife couldn't use him. Crazy games if you have money, I guess. Having handled the monthly finances for years and co-signing the annual tax forms, I had a general idea of what I had to gain but was fairly in the dark regarding the business. I was involved early on, but it got to be too much with my job and raising the children. Nevertheless, the decision was clear after the two consultations. I needed the best, and I definitely got the best. The caveat here is that he charged a $10,000 retainer fee that needed to be paid upfront and my fees went well beyond that after all was said and done. I am telling you this just to prepare you for how expensive things can get. You really need to have a "come-to-Jesus" moment when it comes to deciding on how much you have to gain vs. how much you could stand to lose.

Research/Preparation

While waiting for your consultation appointment, it is imperative that you do your research, especially in context to the different types of divorce, marital split of property, and custody of children. Prepare a list of questions, needs, wants, etc. The lawyer's time is money so you need to be prepared. It will help you expedite the meeting and leave with less fear and more confidence in knowing what to expect. Here's a list of some of the things you would want to be prepared with:

1.   The type of divorce you are asking for
2.   What your husband earns. If he is self-employed, get as much information about his business finances as is possible.
3.   What you earn as well as a realistic appraisal of your earning potential
4.   If you are able to obtain copies of the following documents, it will be extremely helpful:
     i.   Tax returns
     ii.   Bank statements
     iii.   Investment statements
     iv.   College saving accounts
     v.   Retirement accounts
     vi.   Life insurance policies
     vii.   Wills
     viii. Social Security statements
     ix.   Credit card statements
     x.   Healthcare cards
     xi.   Vehicle titles (car, truck, boat, jet ski, trailers, etc.)
     xii.   Email/text correspondence between you and your husband
5.   Know your household budget and expenses. This will include monthly bills: mortgage, HOA fees, utilities, phones and internet, food, gasoline, television services, vehicle payments, insurance payments, healthcare, gym membership, trash

removal, lawn/landscaping services, credit card payments, pest control maintenance, cleaning services, and entertainment (movies, parties, restaurants, fast food, traveling, etc.). Don't forget childcare expenses including daycare/school costs, clothing/shoes, healthcare, cost of activities/equipment (sports, dance, music lessons, theatre, scouts, etc.), and all other expenses related to raising children.

6. Be prepared with a list of your assets:
     i. Home(s)
     ii. Property
     iii. Car(s)
     iv. Boat(s)/fishing gear
     v. Motorcycle(s)
     vi. Jet Ski(s)
     vii. Household possessions/Furniture
     viii. Artwork
     ix. Jewelry
     x. Weapons/ammunition
     xi. Safe deposit boxes
     xii. Anything with monetary value
7. Your wishes for the custody of your children
8. Your wishes for alimony
9. Your wishes for your legal and court costs to be paid by your spouse

Much of what I have listed above, I did not have for my initial consultations and quite honestly, it would have taken me weeks to put all that information together. I was able to offer enough information to give the lawyers a good idea of how time intensive my case would be. Had I known then, what I know now, I would have gone to these consults better prepared. Nonetheless, I was required to produce all of these documents during the Discovery phase of the process and answer pages of questions from my spouse's lawyer. In my case, Discovery took months between obtaining all the documents, answering all the questions, and the multitude of correspondences with my attorney and my spouse's lawyer.

Make no mistake, this was exhausting and took its toll on me, especially when the other side was dealing in mistruths and incomplete document submissions. But you have to dig deep and realize your end goal. You need to be able to take care of your children and yourself. Limiting the impact that divorce has on your children is paramount.

Children First

Profound moment #7

Put your kids at the top of your agenda! Although this is #7 in book progression, it is #1 in order of importance. They are innocent in this. You were given these beautiful human beings! As a parent, you are charged with caring for them, raising them to be independent and respectful, and protecting them. Do not use them as pawns in a game of revenge. It's tempting to want to use them to hurt your husband. Resist that urge with every fiber of your being. You will make mistakes. You will falter. You will hurt them. Recognize your failures, apologize to your kids, and forgive yourself. They love you! They want the two of you to be happy and get along. Your honesty will gain their respect and trust. Remember Karma? Do you want the good one or the bad?

My advice is to keep the routines of your children as normal as possible and do not put them in the middle of your legal battles. Put them first in all that you do during this time. Stay involved. They need you more than ever now.

Settle custody as quickly as possible and avoid frequent changes between homes. Although not always possible, the quicker you can come to an agreement on this, the better it is for a more positive transition for your children. Again, your children are your first priority. No matter how angry you are with your ex-husband for what he has done to you and your family, I will repeat again, your children are not pawns in a game of revenge! You need to make decisions that are in their best interest. Shared custody, 50/50, is usually what is in the best interest of your children, but there are circumstances where that may not be the case. If their father is acting out of character or not fulfilling his commitments to his children's visitation and schedules, or if he puts his new girlfriend and her children before his own, and/or if things that he says or does puts them at an emotional or physical risk, then, by all means, fight for more than just 50/50 for the sake of your children. Just realize that you will need to produce clear proof. This is time-intensive and can include: schedules, emails, texts, and in some cases, testimony from a guardian ad litem. A guardian ad litem is an objective, impartial person (usually an attorney) appointed by the court to act as a representative for a minor child in a contested custody proceeding. He/she investigates solutions that would be in the best interests of the children. You need to understand that this is at your expense.

Really be honest about your emotions. Are you fighting for more custody for revenge and/or more child support? If so, you better rethink some things. If you sincerely believe that your child's physical and/or emotional well-being is in jeopardy, a guardian ad litem is necessary. I would like to offer a warning here regarding your children during and after the divorce process. Do not involve them in the legalities. Divorce is an adult issue and should be left to the adults. Don't put them in a position to choose sides. Unfortunately, this was my scenario. My still husband, at the time, was not thinking clearly. He was going through, what I believe, based on research, a typical mid-life crisis. He was obsessed with his new relationship and his new life. He actually wanted our children to testify in court. I absolutely refused to put my children in the middle and, thank God, the court agreed. The guardian ad litem was able to visit each of our homes, the children's schools, and interview people who had contact with our children as well as interview the children themselves. She then made her recommendations to the court on their behalf. I was so grateful that there was no burden placed on them. Can you imagine the guilt they would carry with them? Please don't put your children in that position. That alone is reason enough to work custody out as amicably and quickly as possible.

Work out schedules with the father of your children. There is so much he said/she said that you need to keep correspondences between you and their father in writing (email, text, etc.). Save and make copies with a date/time stamp. This was arduous and time-intensive, but if I had not done it, I would have had no proof that the schedules weren't being adhered to, commitments were not being met, and agreed upon communications were not occurring. If incidents are not documented, then, in the court's eyes, they didn't happen. The other side will just call you a liar. All of these situations greatly impacted our children and their routines causing them undue anxiety during an already difficult time. I also kept a journal of disconcerting stories that my children would share with me especially if it caused them emotional pain, anger, or anxiety. I was able to share all of this with their lawyer as well as their counselor. My goal was to limit, to the best of my abilities, the disruptions in their lives and mine caused by decisions that were forced upon us.

Lastly, DO NOT badmouth the father of your children. I wouldn't be truthful if I didn't say you will stumble here as well. Work on this one especially hard. There were many times at the beginning that I would speak badly about him in anger in front of the children. It could have been over a condescending text he sent, his daughter's field hockey game that he missed, or forgetting to pick his child up to take her to school and leaving her stranded trying to find a ride. Having to deal with these stresses and the anxieties and hurt verbalized by my children, there were many times I found it hard to hold my tongue. Just remember that after you allow the emotions to subside, apologize to your children and vow to try harder. Your job is to raise your children to respect their elders and that means their father as well.

In all dealings with their father regarding the kids, take the higher road as much as humanly possible. I am telling you that, other than in court, you will get the most bang for your buck with good karma here. Trust me, you will see the rewards of "the higher road." I have more advice regarding your children in a later chapter. I just felt it important to hit some of the highlights here during the pivotal, initial crisis phases of the divorce process.

Taxes

It is a good idea to consult an accountant or tax preparer for potential tax issues that you might face post-divorce. The information you receive here could be a part of your settlement. Be as prepared as possible for anything that is going to cost you money. You need to do your best to minimize the financial burden on yourself after the divorce. After all, why should you suffer financially, especially if the divorce is a result of adultery or him just walking out of the marriage? This was crucial for me. Previously, we filed jointly and our taxes were paid through my husband's company. I had no idea what I would be required to pay in yearly taxes, as head of household, as a result of the settlement that I received. The amount was significant and consequently, I have to pay taxes quarterly. Thank goodness my attorney was astute enough to address this in my court proceedings. This information definitely played a role in how much alimony I received.

Nest Egg

This one could be very difficult, if not impossible, especially if you are suddenly abandoned. For most people whose marriages deteriorate over time, they are more likely to gradually hide money aside in the event that a divorce finally becomes a reality. They have time to prepare for being able to pay monthly bills and legal fees. Being blindsided, as I was, there is no luxury of time to prepare for this scenario. It is even further complicated if your husband controls the finances because it is not uncommon that when tensions flare, he will do his best to cut you off financially. This makes you vulnerable and gives him more bargaining power.

If you have money tucked aside somewhere, you can manage until your lawyer can get you an emergency hearing. Maybe you have family or friends that can help. A word of caution here: I don't recommend this unless you fully intend to pay them back. Losing a family member or good friend over money is never worth it. Don't forget, there are free resources out there. Don't let him intimidate you. As I've said before, a friend of mine was able to access some free legal services through our local courthouse. She was able to talk with debt relief services who offered her great free advice to manage her debt until legal decisions were made. She even reached out to local churches and aid agencies who paid her heat and electric bills for a few months. The resources are out there, and you just need to be courageous enough to reach out.

In my case, I had a steady job and could have afforded to keep the kids and myself afloat but it would have meant major lifestyle changes for the children, which was everything I was trying to avoid for them. In my husband's defense, I was lucky enough that he did right by us in this respect. He continued to deposit his checks into our joint account so I was able to pay our bills. This was a system we were both in agreement with for years since he despised keeping track of and paying the bills. He deposited the checks, as I did mine, and I paid the bills. The bottom line for me was that there was no big savings. During our marriage, if we took a trip, he took a disbursement from the company. If I needed a credit card paid, which was rare, he wrote a check from the money he kept aside for himself. This system worked well for us. Unfortunately, when he walked out, I had no nest egg. I was able to pay the monthly bills but where was I going to get $900 for an attorney consultation and $10,000 for a retainer? Well, I charged the consultation fee on a credit card. In terms of the retainer, I scheduled a meeting with my husband and my parents. At this point, I had learned that everything had to be in writing or witnessed when it came to him. He was quite good at lying and denying that certain things were said or done. This behavior was extremely frustrating and exhausting. Although it was tedious and time-intensive to have to document everything, it came in handy for debunking his lies. My parents knew that they were coming only as a witness as I was going to ask for money for the retainer fee. How demoralizing that I had to ask for money that was rightfully mine! I told my soon to be ex that I scheduled this meeting to discuss issues related to the divorce and I wanted my parents present as witnesses. Shockingly enough, he agreed. Long story short, we all met and I asked for the $10,000 retainer fee. He thought it was absolutely outrageous, but what was he going to say to me in front of my parents knowing that they knew what he had done to me and how cruelly he had done it? It was painful. It was demoralizing. It was scary. But, I was resolute in my goal to ensure that my kids and I were financially stable after all this was over. Because of my courage, this became the first of several wins over the course of my divorce journey.

Court

If settlement negotiations fail regarding asset/debt division, child custody, and/or alimony, the process of taking your case to court begins. Your lawyer will be your guide at this point and the legal bills will begin to quickly add up. You will be responsible for producing large amounts of information for your lawyer and the court, much of which we covered earlier in this chapter. You will be required to answer pages of interrogatories, in writing, which are questions that your spouse's lawyer will want answers to in order to clarify facts. This is doable but extremely overwhelming at times. You will have court dates to determine mediation times, settlement conferences, and trial hearings. There will be countless forms submitted by your lawyer to the court requesting things on your behalf which are known as motions. There are motions of request and there are motions to deny motions made by the other side. These in turn are either granted or denied by the courts. All of this is before your case is even heard. It can be mind-boggling. Let me make it clear: this is not an expeditious process. On the contrary, it is slow and arduous. You will be required to attempt mediation with a third party as well. If all this fails, you will have your case heard in court. In some instances, you have to wait months for your court date and then months after your case is heard for a decision from the judge. Money, money, and more money! If you take this route, you better be sure your financial benefit is worth it.

As I'm sure I have already established, there was nothing simple about my divorce. As a matter of fact, it couldn't have been uglier. I filed for absolute divorce on the grounds of his adultery, two months after he walked out. I found it ironic that he left the relationship but waited for me to file for the divorce. He was more than happy to oblige when he received the papers. What was even more ironic was that he admitted to adultery instead of making me prove it, this after lying about almost everything else. We went to mediation four months after that to try and settle our differences to avoid a trial. Because we were unable to reach agreements, we appeared in court for a two-day trial, five months after mediation. It was two days of testimony from experts on both sides to explain the valuation of the business and its worth, testimony from his business accountants and tax accountants, and hours of testimony from me, my husband, his paramour, and a few of the many character witnesses that showed up on my behalf. It was nerve-wracking to testify but I did so much of the leg work prior to the trial that I didn't realize how prepared I was. Honesty was so important at this time as was not being baited to lose my cool. It's all about being calm, professional, respectful, and in control. The stakes were high. I was fighting for my future financial stability. We finally received a decision from the judge three and a half months later, just about 18 months after I was abandoned.

There was also the issue of child custody going on at the same time. There was a great deal of anxiety from my children that I had to deal with simultaneously. They only knew one home and didn't want to be bouncing back and forth to a place that they felt uncomfortable in. They weren't babies. They were teenagers, except for my youngest, and she was hurt the most, having been friends with the paramour's daughter. Their father had become someone they didn't recognize. He told them that he was getting in touch with his "chi." He would leave them for prolonged periods on his designated weekends with them to be with this other woman and put her children's needs before his own kids' needs. Before any custody battle, I was allowing visitation every other weekend within a month of their father leaving the home. The children wanted the stability of being home during the school week especially since their home was closer to their schools. They also felt comfortable that I was on top of their schedules. They very much needed the parent who they felt was more responsible and dependable during this time. They needed time to process, cope, and transition. Their father petitioned the court to establish custody almost five months later, and my children were appointed a "guardian ad litem", a lawyer to represent them. The custody hearing took place two months later and we had a decision a week after that.

I was granted sole physical custody and shared legal custody with final decision making. The weekend visits continued, we split holidays, and he was allowed three non-consecutive weeks a summer with them. A little over a year and a half after the first custody decision, their father motioned to amend the custody agreement and was denied it by the courts. The children were again appointed a lawyer to speak on their behalf for this proceeding as well. This time around, the kids were livid that they were being put through this intrusion into their lives again. It was agonizing as a parent to see them have to go through this, but they appreciated that I wouldn't stop fighting for what they wanted. Although their father's motion to amend custody was denied, I did allow visitation once a week for dinner. Two years and four months after their father left, the custody fight officially came to a close. After reading all of this drama, I sarcastically ask, "Is my message of arduous processes being received yet?" If not, it's not over yet. I warned you it was ugly.

Let me briefly recap by saying that our divorce was final just about a year and a half after my former husband abandoned me. To make matters worse, he appealed the judge's decision within a week. This required further information sharing, further attempts at mediation and settlement, depositions, and a hearing before three judges at the Appellate Court before the case was put back to our original presiding judge for him to make whatever changes he felt appropriate based on the recommendations of the appellate court. We received that decision a little over three years after my ex appealed. Just to put this in perspective, I spent four years of my life dealing with the legal system. Grant it, mine was ugly but what I gained surely outweighed the expenses. My honesty, strength, and perseverance got me what I rightfully deserved, especially in terms of taking care of my children. I will say that I tried valiantly to settle at every phase of this four-year process and he refused. As a result, I was granted more than I was willing to settle for in the initial divorce proceedings and I was granted more than I was willing to settle for after the appellate process.

To restate this chapter's title, bad karma's a bitch. He literally paid for his bad karma as a result of his many lies from the beginning to the end. My advice to you is to do your best NOT to be on the wrong side of the statement, "Karma's a Bitch." I am here to tell you that good karma prevails. At this point, you are still hurt, angry, and bitter. These emotions make normal activities of daily living seem almost impossible. These emotions also cloud judgment and decision-making. No one understands this more than me. Don't do anything stupid, like sending nasty emails or texts. Don't create scenes in public. There should be no harassment of any kind. Stupid could come back and bite you in the ass in court. In order for you to obtain the best possible outcome, you need to dig deep for positive thinking. You need to do everything you are asked to do by your lawyer as thoroughly and on time as possible. Rule following has never been more important than now. Taking the higher road as much as possible without hurting your case is paramount. Most of all, be HONEST at all points in the process. You will stay in your boat! You will stay afloat! And you will be the best damn Captain anyone has ever seen!!! **You've got this!**

Chapter 5: Kids Need a Parent, Not a Friend

As if struggling with your emotions and the legalities of your divorce weren't enough, you may have children to deal with as well. As I discussed with **Profound Moment #7**, they need to be your focus both during and after the divorce. Under normal circumstances, children have emotional and physical issues that need to be met. During and after your divorce, you will face even more challenges with respect to your children. It is important that they be able to trust you and count on you to get them through. Your time and attention are in short supply with everything that you have going on but this is exactly what they need and you need to work extra hard to give it to them.

Truer words were never spoken than those in the title of this chapter. Whether married or divorced, you are a parent first and this is especially true during the divorce and after. The research regarding parenting during divorce is very clear, almost like a rule book of sorts. Quite frankly, an entire book can be written on this topic alone. For the purpose of surviving the initial crisis and beyond, several do's and don'ts will be shared along with some more profound moments. Educate yourself. Read books, read articles on websites, or even seek professional help if necessary. Being aware of how divorce will impact your children and how you respond, is critical in how well they will cope and adapt. My ex and I had court ordered parenting classes that we were required to attend. Although most of it was common sense, I was grateful for the information, particularly because we were both doing some of the don'ts. I also had my kids in counseling almost immediately. Because they were older, compounded by the fact that their father's departure was so unexpected and his relationship was with someone they knew, they needed help, and as did I, to assist them in coming to terms with their emotions and the consequences of their father's decision.

Do not assume that your kids are strong and resilient. Most people think older children are mature enough to handle the divorce of their parents. I would beg to differ. My kids were crushed. At first there was disbelief, then, there was anger not only with the situation but with the changes and inconveniences that it brought into their lives. Although they loved their father, they despised packing their bags and going to another house every other weekend to stay with people that they were uncomfortable with. They were absolutely not about and are still not about the "one big happy family" notion. They want their time with their father and only him. Being teenagers, they quickly learned the power of manipulation.

Your children's understanding of your divorce will evolve as they get older. It is of utmost importance that you make it very clear to your children that the end of your marriage is not the end of the relationship between them and you or between them and their relationship with their father. You will need to emphasize that both parents will always love them. As it is not an easy time for you, this will certainly not be an easy time for them with all of the changes and transitions. There can be definite feelings of abandonment. Unfortunately, I was left to deal with the emotional fallout during the initial months and years after their father left. He was too busy with his new life. He went from parenting and disciplining on the same page with me, as we had done for 16 years, to a parenting style with zero discipline. Based on the stories that the children would convey to me, most of their conversations with their father surrounded his need for them to accept his girlfriend and her kids. It was an astonishingly difficult time for them and me. The message here is that, no matter what, you need to make them feel safe, secure, and loved. You have the capacity to save your children from the damaging impact of your divorce.

Stable Transition for your Children

Be nurturing, supportive, firm, and present. This is when children need you the most. Spend time with each of them individually each day. Ask them what they think and feel but don't always expect or require an answer. Just make sure they know you want and are willing to listen. Quality time with your kids is important. Easier said than done you say. "I can barely function to keep myself together as I deal with the overwhelming feelings of anger, grief, and sadness. How can I possibly be effective when my kids can see that I'm an obvious mess?" Again, it is time to dig deep. Your children need to come first. Put a daily reminder to spend time talking with your kids, either on your phone or on your bathroom mirror or both. With everything you say and before every decision you make, consider the effect it will have on your children. This could even help you deal with your negative emotions in a better way. When you can justify taking the higher road for the sake of your children, it lessens the anger and bitterness because you know, logically, that how you feel about your ex is less important than how you act toward him in the eyes of your children.

Create routines and schedules. Children of all ages benefit from consistency. Keeping them as close to their normal routines and schedules as possible reinforces their sense of security during the transitions of divorce. Our kids were very involved in school activities and athletics. Their schedules were full. The children's father and I had a shared calendar that we created through an app. I would put all of the activities and appointments in it as well as when the kids were to be in his care. Our vacation weeks and holiday schedules were added as well. We even put in when each of us was not available for the kids.

You will also need to provide clear rules and limits while using consistent discipline. This one is extremely important and probably the most frustrating and difficult. While you may have thought that you parented fairly consistently and remained on the same page when you were married, you might find this changing after divorce. While most of the child care decisions were left to one parent during the marriage, after divorce, the other parent finds that he or she didn't always agree with the decisions that were made and is no longer concerned with keeping the peace. This creates confusion for children when one consistent parenting style now becomes two, sometimes very different, parenting styles. This disconnect, usually, gives rise to some significant challenges for your kids.

In many cases, mine included, my ex and I were always on the same page with parenting when we were married. It was "What did your mother say or what did your father say?" We tried at all costs to avoid our kids pitting us against each other by always presenting a united front. After the divorce, I continued to be the parent and he tried to be their friend. He was the "fun guy," the "Disneyland dad" while I was the disciplinarian, the "bad guy." This caused a whole host of issues with the kids which included some 'acting-out' behaviors and manipulative behaviors aimed at pitting their father and me against each other to get what they wanted. While each of you has the right to develop your own parenting style, you need to consider what your children are accustomed to and develop a style that maintains consistency and limits harm.

Profound Moment #8

This brings us **to Profound Moment #8**. You are your children's parent, not their friend. No matter what age, your kids will test you, again and again, and then again. It's okay to be the "bad guy." As a matter of fact, own it! They will give you a hard time, act out, and try to manipulate you! Stick to your guns. I promise you that they will not stop loving you. Oftentimes you may wait years for the payoff of being the 'bad guy,' but it will be worth it. Not to mention, your children will benefit by being more responsible, caring, trustworthy, and respectful adults. After all, those are our ultimate goals, right?

End the conflict with your children's father. Do not let your feelings dictate your behavior. Kids adjust more easily when parents show a healthy sense of respect for each other, despite difficult circumstances. Having said that, the opposite is a far more common reality, especially during the initial phases of the separation and divorce process. As I've said in the previous chapter, this is where we stumble the most. We vent to others about our ex when the children are in earshot; we bad-mouth him in our anger; and we use our kids as messengers to pass along information. Again, these are a NO, a NO and a NO. Catch yourself, apologize to your children, and promise to try harder. Don't underestimate the power of an apology, especially to your children. They need to know that you are not perfect and that you are willing to admit your faults. It shows them that you understand the hurt you caused them and that you respect and love them enough to try to repair the damage done to the relationship. The more aware you become of your criticisms, the more quickly you will recognize and stop yourself and the faster you will eliminate these behaviors for the sake of your children.

Profound Moment #9

Ending conflict between you and the father of your children is so important that it deserves the **Profound Moment #9** status. Let's recap the things that will help you do just that:

- o Be kid focused. Your children's well-being comes first.
- o How you feel about your ex is less important than how you act toward him.
- o Do not vent about your ex to the children when they are in earshot.
- o Do not put your kids in the middle. They are not to be the messengers between the two of you. You shouldn't place them in a position of deciding between the two of you on any issue.
- o If you cannot resolve conflict, you may need help from a professional. Your children may require counseling as well, as this will definitely affect them mentally and emotionally.

Support your children's relationships with their father and his extended family. No matter how difficult it may seem, you must acknowledge what their father has to offer. Remember, you were married to him. There were qualities that attracted you to him. There were reasons your marriage lasted so long. These qualities benefited you during your marriage and they will benefit your children, as well, moving forward. I completely understand how difficult this is when you are hurt and can't see beyond the pain. It was extremely difficult for me, especially early on. From the start, no matter how much it hurt, I knew our kids needed their father. I would encourage them to go to the weekly dinners and keep their weekend visits commitment even when they didn't want to go. I would express my happiness when they had a good visit with him. I would tell them how much their father loved them even when they felt that they came second to his girlfriend and her children. I encouraged them to continue to speak with him about their frustrations even when they felt like he wasn't listening. I would make positive comments about their physical characteristics that they inherited from their father, the personality traits that they got from him, or something that they did that I was proud of and reminded me of him. Were there snarky remarks made by me on many occasions? Of course. Was I proud of that? Of course not. It was difficult to reign in the bitterness at times, and my children got pretty good at calling me out on it. This honestly helped me to stop or at least keep it to a bare minimum. I will tell you when I did muster the effort to foster a better relationship between my children and their father, it was somehow freeing and felt like progress. I was proud of myself. I will also tell you that this gets easier as time passes by. Be patient with yourself.

Don't forget that the kids have developed bonds with his side of the family, not just yours. You need to encourage and foster these relationships even if you have to be the one to arrange these get-togethers because your ex is too distracted or self-absorbed. Is it going to feel awkward and uncomfortable? Absolutely! I set up dinner dates for the kids and my ex's parents. We kept in touch through letters. I would send them a yearly calendar with different pictures of the kids on each month. The more efforts you make, the easier it gets. These bonds are just as important to his family as they are to your children. Yes, you must again swallow your pride and take the higher road.

Profound Moment #10

As this "take the higher road" seems to be a repetitive theme, it is time to give it the profound moment designation. **Profound Moment #10** is to take the higher road whenever possible, for self-preservation as well as for the sake of your children. You ask, "How many times do I need to take the higher road?" You want to scream, "Why am I always the one who has to take the damn higher road?!" Unfortunately, all I can tell you is that it won't be the last time. You will be amazed at the strength you have when it comes to protecting your kids and doing what is best for them. As a woman, it is instinctual; there is no denying it. I will also reiterate that there is exceptionally good karma that results from taking the higher road. Amen to that, am I right?! Nevertheless, just do it! It's the right thing to do and deep down you know it.

Do not burden your kids with adult responsibilities. You are the adult; they are the children. They should not be your confidants nor your companions. You should never disclose adult information such as divorce proceedings, custody disagreements, finances, child support, and/or alimony details. This can have detrimental effects on the emotional well-being of your children. This happened in my case. My ex pressured the kids with custody issues and actually told them how much he was giving me for child support and alimony. Again, my children were 16, 13, and 11. Not extremely young by any means, but at no age, when your child is a minor, can you expect them to comprehend such issues. In my case, the children had a lot of anxiety during the custody disagreements between their father and me. They didn't want to hurt either of us. I think having their own lawyer to speak to was Godsend for them. In their eyes, she could be the bad guy for delivering the message of what they wanted. As for being told about alimony and child support numbers, they just knew numbers and not the meaning behind them. And since they were teenagers, I had to deal with their disappointments when they didn't get the materialistic things they wanted. In their selfish attempts to manipulate me to get what they wanted, they each, individually, at one point or another, would verbalize to me the financial numbers they were told. They didn't understand that child support was also about maintaining their standard of living, feeding and clothing them, keeping a roof over their head, paying for all of their activities and entertainment, paying for travel, paying for cars and car insurance, etc. Whatever money that wasn't used for them was invested into accounts for their future to pay for my half of their college tuition, weddings, etc. The money would be theirs, no matter what. We didn't raise our kids to get whatever they wanted when they wanted it and I wasn't going to start then. This caused quite a bit of unnecessary drama that would have never occurred had this information not been shared with them. Their father and I grew up in loving families that lived paycheck to paycheck. We built a great life and earned every bit of what we had with hard work. Our children had no idea what we had because we wanted them to work hard to be able to appreciate what they earned, not have it handed to them. They had no idea what we had until numbers were put in their heads. Unfortunately, their father's poor decision to give the children this type of information not only put them in the middle but caused them to question each of us unnecessarily with the result being them not knowing who to believe. It shattered the very stability and security that I was trying to achieve. Anger and bitterness run high on both sides during divorce but under no circumstance is this ever in the best interest of your children. These are adult issues and need to be worked through by the adults.

If you find yourself in a situation similar to mine, it's best not to stoop to that level or add any more fuel to the fire. You are tempted to defend yourself because not doing so, makes you appear to be the guilty party, the "bad guy," again, in the eyes of your children. But let's put this in perspective. If you defend yourself, you add to your kids' confusion, you put them further in the middle, and you further alienate them because they don't know who to believe. Now their ability to trust is impacted, and they feel even less secure. Is this what you want for them? Of course you don't! I have to admit, this one took its toll. It went on for four years throughout the divorce process, the divorce appeal process, and the custody appeal process. There came a time when the children were no longer minors, and the issues of child support and alimony continued to be thrown in their faces by their father when I finally explained the details of the decisions made by the judge. I explained the finances and the reasons for the child support and alimony amounts; I explained what the monies were used for and how some of it was invested for them and their futures. I made the court documents available for them to read so they could see the truth if they desired to. I also provided them with information on their accounts and investments. They were ready at that point, and were old enough to read and comprehend the court documents and the financial information. Is it unfortunate that my children had to endure this emotional abuse? Most definitely. But I was able to limit the damage by not engaging with the issue when they were too young to understand. I allowed myself to be "thrown under the bus" for the well-being of my children. It wasn't the first time, and it wouldn't be the last. Knowing that they didn't know the real truth was agonizing. It hurt me as they believed lies about their mother. But I knew the truth would eventually come out, and that, along with doing right by my kids, was what got me through. I will tell you that they never did choose to read the court documents, probably because they were so lengthy but I'm hoping it was also, in part, because they trusted and believed in me. My sincere advice is to avoid my experience if at all possible. Let your kids be kids. They deserve that much. They will be grown-ups soon enough.

Seek out sources of social support for your children. Their friends and family are important. It is vital that they continue with the activities that they have been involved in. If you find that your kids are having problems coping with the changes they are experiencing, never hesitate to seek professional help. There is no shame. On the contrary, it could be life-changing and/or even life-saving. I found it necessary for myself and my children during the initial months of crisis and throughout the first year. Although, they might not agree and could tell you, to this day, that they hated it and that it was unnecessary, I am assuring you that it was not. Counseling is especially critical, if you see clear signs of emotional or physical abuse. I have no regrets seeking professional help and feel that it was extremely beneficial for my children as well as for myself. Having this unbiased person to listen and help the children more effectively work through the transition and the confusion was comforting for them, comforting for me, and ultimately paved the way for them to confidently express their feelings and develop some constructive coping strategies to deal with the stresses that were inevitably placed upon them by both their parents.

Co-Parenting

Co-parenting is the most beneficial for your children if much of what has already been discussed is incorporated. Once primary residential custody has been decided, then, if legal custody is shared, joint decisions can be made regarding religion, education, physical health, finances, recreation, emergencies, morality, etc. A co-parenting plan will then need to be developed and should include how you will handle and divide the daily activities. There are several helpful co-parenting tips and you will find that they mirror those in the transition checklist.

- Setting aside hurt and anger is paramount if you wish to remain child focused. Again, when it comes to the kids, how you feel about their father is less important than how you act toward him.

- Peaceful, consistent and purposeful communication with the co-parent is key. Texts and emails should be business-like. Make requests, not demands. Listen, show restraint, and keep the conversations solely focused on the children. You could find it helpful, as I did, to create a shared electronic calendar that outlines the children's activities, their appointments, the visitation schedules, the kids' vacation weeks, and even when each parent was unavailable or out of town. It was convenient that we were each able to see it and make changes to it. There is even the ability to set up alerts when additions and/or changes are made.

- The goal is to co-parent as a team. Be as consistent as possible between households regarding rules, homework, curfews, off-limit activities, and discipline. Make important decisions regarding the kids together. Resolve disagreements while respecting each other and without involving the children. Learning to compromise is the most challenging and you really need to learn to not sweat the small stuff.

- Make the transitions between households as easy as possible. This will definitely decrease the anxiety of the children. Remember, each hello is also a goodbye for your kids. Remind them, a day or two in advance, when they will be going to their father's so they can mentally prepare and pack in advance. Keep to the visitation schedule laid out by the custody agreement. This prevents your kids from having undue guilt when they leave each parent. Also realize that your ex's time with the kids is just as sacred as your time with them. Do not change the drop off or pick up times or plan things during the other's time. It is also important to allow your children space when they return from their father. Do not hound them with questions about their visit.
- Respect your need for privacy. The only information that needs to be shared between co-parents is that pertaining to the children.

Understand that custody was a huge battle for me for the first two years. As a result, co-parenting was not easy. There was anger and bitterness on both sides. It was easy for me to be a responsible parent. I had always adhered to schedules and ensured that my kids did their homework, abided by curfews, and had consequences for irresponsible behavior. I continued to do so even after the divorce. Unfortunately, I had to deal with a difficult co-parent. The road was rocky, but we made it through, and I am very proud of who our kids have become. It is important to understand that your co-parenting plan will change as your children grow and mature, and it will be up to both of you to revisit the plan on occasion and make changes accordingly. The plan did change for us as the children matured and it also got easier, as they became more independent.

There have been clearly documented benefits of co-parenting for children:

- Children feel secure.
- Kids benefit from consistency.
- They better understand problem-solving.

- A healthy example is set for children to follow.
- Children are mentally and emotionally healthier.

It's a no brainer folks. Isn't this what we want for our babies?!

Dealing with a Difficult Co-Parent

Unfortunately, I did have to deal with a difficult co-parent. There were no rules when the kids were in his care. He even admitted that in court. The children were rarely picked up and dropped off on time. There was no discipline for bad behavior. He failed to follow through with court ordered communications between us. He would cancel weekly dinners with the kids at the last minute. He would cancel or forget his commitment to take his youngest daughter to school on preset days of the week. The list is lengthy. All of these not only made my job as a parent harder but created a ripe environment for teenage manipulation. It was extremely hard when they would try to pit us against each other for their personal gain. I was the bad guy because I always stuck to my guns. It was heart-wrenching, but I knew my kids needed boundaries and one day they would appreciate me for it. And guess what? As responsible adults, they do appreciate me and love me dearly as I do them.

As you are all very well aware, it is extremely difficult to cooperate and negotiate when emotions are running high. It is very easy to sink to each other's level and make decisions that might not be in the best interest of your children. Remember **Profound Moment #10**, take the higher road. Don't engage in dead-end arguments but instead stress that you are interested in communicating about what is best for the kids. Continuing a vicious circle of ugly helps no one and creates more unnecessary anxiety and anger. If you do happen to be in a situation where you have a pending court case, keep records of all interactions and communications:

1. Are they keeping their commitments regarding custody and visitation?

2. Are they providing consistent, positive messages to the children?
3. If they are refusing to keep to the custody schedule or if they are putting the kids at physical or emotional risk, consult your lawyer and/or child protective agencies and be able to provide solid proof of your accusations.

Additional Don'ts Regarding your Children

I've compiled an additional list of actions that are damaging and counterproductive for your children. I'm sure that you have already experienced many of these. Consider this your wake-up call because if you do not heed to them, your behavior with your kids will backfire and create more misery for you in the future. So, you need to be diligent and firm.

1. Don't try and buy your kids' love or give them what they want out of guilt. You will only create self-entitled and ungrateful monsters.
2. Don't try to "one up" your ex when it comes to the children. Kids are fairly selfish; it's all about them. They learn very quickly from this behavior and behavior #1 how to manipulate you and pit you against their father to get what they want.
3. Stick to the terms of the custody agreement or you will eventually be played by your children and/or your ex when they don't get their way.
4. Kids will say very hurtful things and try and use guilt trips when they are angry with you or don't get what they want. You better grow a thick skin, quick, ladies! And by all means, call them out on their behavior and demand respect as their mother.
5. Don't seem uninterested when your children want to share the good things that happened when they were with their father, but then, be all about the 50 questions when they share something negative that happened during their visit. Although tempting, I'll admit, do not engage. Be happy for their good times and acknowledge them and refrain from relishing in and perpetuating the negatives they express

about their father. Instead, listen and offer positive advice to aid them in dealing with the issues that are causing them distress. They are venting out of a need for assistance, not for agreement and further bashing.

6. Do not give your children a guilt trip. You are a mature adult and game-playing should not be in your repertoire, especially when it comes to your kids. This just results in your children learning unhealthy coping habits.

7. There comes a time when your children are old enough for conversations regarding boundaries. By this, I mean that sometimes, your kids can share too much about their father, TMI so to speak. The kind of TMI that opens old wounds and changes your mood. Self-preservation is not always a bad thing. Your children aren't mind-readers and don't always know unless you communicate these boundaries clearly. Many times, they figure out for themselves what sets you off and sometimes it requires a conversation. Trust me, just as they say, "a happy wife means a happy life," your kids also know "if mom ain't happy, ain't nobody happy." They will be more than amenable to comply with your wishes, unless of course, they are angry with you and want to hurt you by using TMI in retaliation. If this is the case, refer back to #4 and deal with your child's behavior accordingly.

Bottom line, Be a Parent, Not a Friend. Your children need a strong, consistent, dependable, supportive, caring, loving parent, and role-model at a time when, like you, it is arguably one of the most difficult times in their lives. YOU ARE THAT PARENT! BE THAT PARENT! **You've got this!**

Chapter 6: The Stranglehold of Anger and Bitterness

Yes, we are re-visiting this one. Anger and bitterness don't go away that easily. They are like the annoying meal that keeps repeating on you or like the pesky fly during a picnic. You just can't control when it arises, and it keeps coming back no matter how many times you swat it away. Therefore, it definitely warrants another look, but this time around, let's look at it in the context of beyond, what I call, the crisis phase of a divorce. No matter how much you think you are over it and have moved on with your life, there seems to be triggers that cause these feelings to rear their ugly heads. I have good news, and I have bad news. I apologize but I'm a "bad news first" kind of gal, always feeling as though ending with the positive somehow makes dealing with it easier. So, bad news: you may be living with these emotions for years; good news: you will no longer be consumed by them.

Although losing a spouse from divorce is very similar to losing a spouse to death, there are some differences. The first being that your ex is still alive and, for some, unfortunately so. Second, the feelings of anger and bitterness take a different path than those resulting from death. This stranglehold that I refer to can be frustrating, disappointing and discouraging. You've already been through the denial, the anger, the depression and the acceptance. You can hear yourself saying, "Why am I allowing the resentment to still be triggered? Why does it sometimes seem out of my control? How do I make it stop so that I can feel like I've truly moved on once and for all?"

This emotional struggle was difficult for me because it was a four-year battle between child custody and divorce. After about a year, my anger and bitterness were less about the affair and destruction of our family and more about what my ex was putting me through, legally and what he was putting the kids through, emotionally. There was the barrage of legal correspondences, anxiety over court proceedings, our kids needing a lawyer intruding in their lives not once but twice, the frustrations of an irresponsible co-parent, and the biggest was the multitude of times the kids came to me hurt that they were second to his girlfriend's children. I dealt with incidents surrounding these issues almost daily and at the very least, weekly. My struggle with controlling my frustrations was substantial. It took a great deal of effort on my part but I did it through counseling, exercise, yoga, meditation and journaling. I did a great deal of positive thinking exercises, which included rereading sections of The Secret, creating a vision board with a collage of motivational images, and journaling about my strength to persevere.

Although our children had and have addressed their frustrations with their father many times, his behaviors have not changed. These were the issues that occupied my thoughts and continued to fuel my resentment for years. However, after the court battles ended and my children were able to speak up more effectively for themselves, I would rarely get affected by these emotions. Surprisingly enough, they still come to me with disappointment that his girlfriend's children's needs come before theirs. I get a twinge of annoyance in these instances, but the emotions are much less intense. My kids are able to fight their own battles now. More than anything, it's more of a heartbreaking emotion for me now that they still have to deal with this pain after so many years. The children have learned to love him as he is, accept him where he is and move on. They find that this limits their hurt. They now have the maturity and the power to choose which battles to fight and which ones to leave because they will be a waste of time and energy.

Triggers

At this point, you will be fairly aware of what triggers your anger or bitterness and if you are not, I'm sure that family members, friends, and especially your kids will be more than happy to point them out for you. Once you've hit this point in the process, most of your triggers will have to do with your children. Whether they speak positively about their father or negatively, your resentment will be activated. Aside from issues relating to your children, you may also be triggered by incidents such as seeing your ex on social media, running into one of his coworkers, seeing your ex or his significant other in public, or simply having to share important milestones with your children.

The two most incendiary triggers that I dealt with for several years after the divorce surrounded my frustrations with having to deal with a difficult co-parent as well as him bringing his girlfriend to the children's events, in particular, those events that her children were not a part of. Addressing the first, there was blatant refusal to honor the commitments of the custody agreement when it came to visitation pick up and drop off times. He would make schedule changes or cancel commitments by only notifying the kids. These changes ultimately affected me and my schedule yet I was never communicated with. Two years after he walked out, we still had occasional counseling sessions because he refused to communicate with me when it came to the children. To address the latter, you can only imagine what the site of the girlfriend did to me. Every time I see her, even to this day, a fire burns inside of me. I can't get past the fact that she was a willing participant in breaking up my family and hurting my children while not only pretending to be my friend but also knowing for two years that it was a happy family. Initially, my irritation came in the form of angry outbursts to my children followed by texts or emails to their father conveying my frustrations with his irresponsible parenting and lack of communication. The outbursts were unfair to my children and the emails and texts to my ex never ended well either. They just snowballed into us hoisting insults and threats at each other. Counseling helped a bit as did our kids growing older. As they matured and were able to drive, they were better equipped to wage their own battles with their father and choose their own schedules.

Please understand that these feelings are perfectly normal. Don't beat yourself up about it. Each triggering event will have to be dealt with individually. There are many coping strategies offered in Chapter 2 that might be useful for you to manage these feelings. I used all of them. Depending on the severity of your emotions, counseling may be necessary, especially if you are feeling that you are not making any progress over time. These feelings can, and usually do, last for years but should no longer be all-consuming. Counseling is never a bad option and is always valuable. It was certainly impactful for me. It is extremely important not to take your anger and bitterness about your ex out on your children. As I've stated before, you will make mistakes but it is essential that you recognize it, apologize to your children, and communicate that you will try harder to make sure it doesn't happen again. It might not be the last time you falter when it comes to your kids but they deserve your remorse and your honesty. It conveys your love and desire for their well-being and protection. Last but not least, and for God's sake, if you haven't already done so, delete your ex from all of your social media! It will only cause you more pain to see pictures of him, his new relationship, and his happiness in his new life while you wallow in yours. Why would you inflict such pain on yourself? He no longer holds a place in your life other than as the father of your children, if you have any. Trying to keep tabs on him only serves as another trigger for more resentment. I strongly recommend that you delete, delete, and delete.

Forgiveness: Yes or No?

This can be quite the dilemma. "What does it mean to forgive someone?" "Can I forgive someone and not be on speaking terms with them?" "How can I forgive when I still hurt inside?" "Is forgiveness necessary for my health?" "What if I just can't forgive?" These are all common questions that you will struggle with at some point or at multiple points when forgiveness just doesn't seem like an option. There has been great debate over whether true forgiveness requires positive feelings toward the person who hurt you. After some research, I've decided to include information from several sources and you can do with it as you wish. You are the only one who can decide what the best decision will be for you and your journey.

Psychologists generally define forgiveness as a conscious, deliberate decision to release feelings of resentment or vengeance toward a person or group who has harmed you regardless of whether they actually deserve your forgiveness. They also go on to state that forgiveness does not mean excusing or condoning the offenses. Another source proclaims that you can forgive someone and not talk to them because to forgive a person is about you, not them. It frees you from corrosive anger so that you can heal and move on. It doesn't mean you have to keep them in your life. Forgiveness requires the feeling of willing to forgive. You may not be willing because the hurt went too deep or because the person expressed no regret or remorse. It is probably not in the best interest of your mental health to forgive someone before you have identified, fully felt, expressed, and released your anger and pain. Some say forgiveness transforms people from victims to survivors, from helpless to empowered. One common but mistaken belief, according to mental health professionals, is that forgiveness means letting the person who hurt you off the hook. This is not the case. Again, this is about you and your well-being not the person who hurt you. Research has shown that forgiveness is linked to reduced anxiety, stress, depression, and major psychiatric disorders. It is also associated with fewer physical health symptoms and lower mortality rates. You must accept that forgiveness is not about changing the other person, their actions, or their behaviors. Forgiveness does not mean trust. If you just cannot forgive, don't think that you are a bad person or that you failed in some way. In some cases, forgiveness is just not possible. You may learn not to despise your ex but saying you forgive can be hollow if that is not what you truly feel.

For me, this decision is still a struggle. I grapple with the hurt that there was never any remorse and that the lives of my children are forever changed. Although my children are now well adjusted, for which I am grateful, they will forever be a bit jaded with respect to relationships, love, trust, faith in humanity, and much more. I'm not confident that some feelings of anger and bitterness won't still arise for me, on occasion (and I think you would be lying to yourself if you said you would forever be totally free from it). However, I do believe that I am free of the corrosiveness of these emotions, and I have figured out how to effectively manage them. I do feel like a survivor at this point in my life, and I am amazingly empowered. Does this mean I have forgiven? Maybe? Will I ever say the words aloud to my ex? Probably not! But, as they say, never say never. And for this reason, I don't believe that I have truly forgiven. But surprisingly, I do think that my positive growth has been nothing less than miraculous. Neither my mental health nor my physical health is suffering. I no longer have any stress or anxiety resulting from the loss of my marriage or the uncertainty of my future. I am excited to embrace what comes next. As more time passes, will I say the words and mean them? Maybe. Again, deciding not to forgive is not what I am suggesting. I'm merely sharing my experience as well as the literature. I suggest whatever is best for promoting your healing and your progress. That's what is most important.

Profound Moment #11

Let's recap with **Profound Moment #11**. Get a good handle on your anger and bitterness. This is your time for positive personal growth! Effectively tackling these emotions is pivotal for a positive transition. Begin to remember the good times you and your ex shared, and believe me, there were many. Share these fun, exciting, and loving moments with your children, your family and your friends when the opportunities present themselves. Appreciate what you had and have in your life. Keep your faith in humanity! You have many more exhilarating moments ahead of you! **You've got this!**

Chapter 7: From Caterpillar to Butterfly: Your Transformation

The very moment you were abandoned marked the beginning of your transformation. It just didn't seem very apparent as you struggled through your emotions and the legal system. Once the divorce is final and you've learned to reign in your emotions, you become more aware of the strong and independent person that you are becoming.

I had a solid two years to figure out how to do it all on my own, how to grieve and cope with my emotions, how to deal with the emotions of my kids during the transitions, and figure out who I was again. I became someone I was proud of, not only for myself, but for the positive role model I had become for my children. I was very lucky during this time to have an incredibly supportive family and amazing friends. I was always included in plans and was never made to feel like a third wheel. This was my time to try new things, travel with my kids and by myself, and actually be able to go out and socialize. Besides my career, I even began volunteer work. Don't be afraid to reach out if you are feeling lonely or having a bad day. Invite friends or family out; the worst they can say is no. Then, you just treat yourself to a glass of wine at home, or a movie, or driving golf balls. Get yourself out and don't sit at home feeling sorry for yourself. This is your transformation. Who is the person you want to be?

Life on Your Own

By now, you've figured out quite a bit about life on your own. Whether you had to relocate or were lucky enough to stay in your home, it's all up to you now. You budget and pay your own bills, you work and arrange childcare, you manage the activities and schedules of your kids and you have become a do-it-yourselfer (D-I-Y) with home projects. Life is busy and overwhelming at times, but you are actually beginning to feel proud of yourself and your accomplishments.

It was the little things that I conquered that inspired me the most. I was so proud of myself when I figured out how to restart my furnace by bleeding the oil through to the boiler system. It was with the help of an online video but I did it! You should have seen me jumping around the house and cheering for myself. I'm glad you didn't though. I probably looked ridiculous. Over the course of time, I figured out how to change out a light switch, how to install outdoor lights, how to restring my grass string trimmer, how to use and maintain my grass cutting tractors, how to change batteries in the jet ski and tractors, and basic things like changing furnace filters, putting things together and patching and painting walls. The more I conquered, the more empowered I became. The things I was not able to physically do or figure out how to do, I hired someone to do it for me when I could afford it or there were friends who would help me.

Coping

At this point, you might or might not have your emotions under control and either way it's okay. I continued with counseling for over two years. This was more about me verbalizing my frustrations resulting from having a difficult co-parent as well as dealing with teenagers who were acting out as a result of it. Again, counseling is not for everyone but can be considered if you find that your emotions are overwhelming. If you find yourself getting depressed or if you just don't feel that you are transitioning in a positive way, do consider it.

Socializing with friends and taking care of yourself still remain important as you continue to transition and transform. I make a concerted effort to spend time with my friends at least once a week, whether it be with one friend or several. We go out for dinner and drinks, or I have them come over to my home. My friends have been critical to my positive transformation.

Taking care of yourself should also remain a priority for you. Spin biking, yoga, and meditation continue to be a big part of my life. I get facials and manicure/pedicures once a month. I continue to journal and update my vision board, both of which inspire me for what I want next and make me grateful for all that I currently have. Faith remains a constant in my life as well. I pray every night and attend church just about every Sunday. It brings me hope. It brings me strength. And it brings me peace.

Career

Whether or not your divorce forces you into a job change, there will be challenges. Obviously, if you do have to make a job change, the unknown, at this point in your life, can be frightening. Maybe you hadn't worked outside the home and now you must or maybe you have to change jobs to make more money or to make your job work with childcare. If you are fortunate enough not to be forced to switch jobs, you might still have to make adjustments for childcare, the kids' activities or even adding hours to increase the income. It can be extremely stressful. Do what you need to do as long as it's legal, of course. The more successful you are at transitioning here, the more positive impact it will have for your future.

I was fortunate in my career as a nurse. I primarily worked 12-hour night shifts during the marriage so that I was home for the children during the day. I was sleep-deprived for years, but it worked for us. After the divorce, I needed to be home at night with the children. They were older, but if I wasn't fearing a house fire when I wasn't home, I was fearing a teenage party at my home, the consequences of someone leaving intoxicated and my resulting liability. These fears forced me to move to 12-hour day shifts, which resulted in a pay cut since I no longer received shift differential. I also had to depend more on their father and my friends to help with getting the children to and from their afterschool activities. It was an adjustment for all of us but we persevered. Was it scary? Hell yeah, it was scary but I did it and you, too, have what it takes.

Children

Those of you who have children know that they are forever a part of your life, no matter how old they get. They, too, play a large part in your transformation. Their needs, their desires, their happiness, and their sadness are constantly changing from day to day and sometimes hour to hour. A large part of our lives is devoted to raising our children. They are transforming along with you after the divorce. They will require your continued time, attention, and discipline.

In my case, we traveled a great deal together after the divorce. Our adventures took us to local places, to other cities and states, to islands and coasts and even other countries. We depended on each other and worked together. We navigated airports and unknown places. We planned and executed itineraries. We tried new foods and new experiences. We saw incredibly beautiful places and landscapes. Our bonds became even stronger. Even though we became a family of four, we were still a family nonetheless.

The teenage years were in full swing so there was continued drama to contend with. There were poor decisions with resulting punishments. There were teenage attitudes with parental disrespect. There were also manipulative behaviors with the intent of getting what they wanted. When the children were young, I feared that I would be a naïve parent when they were teenagers since I was a fairly easy and obedient adolescent. Nope. I handled it like a champ. I was tough but fair, firm but loving. My kids will tell you to this day that they are scared of me at times. Some of their friends are too. I guess that means I did my job as a parent.

Self-Discovery

This is perhaps the most exciting part of your transformation. Let's face it, you have spent much of your mid-life sacrificing for your former husband and your children. Now it's time to realize all that you can do by yourself.

You will accomplish a great deal more as you discover who you are again and who you are becoming after your divorce. Take your time. Figure out the person you are and the person you want to be. Get out there and socialize. Travel if you can afford to. Try new things. Develop a hobby. Do what makes you happy. Maybe even start dating if you are ready.

When I look back and see what I was able to accomplish on my own, it is astounding. Besides my D-I-Y projects and traveling with the kids, I also became courageous enough to travel by myself. Although, at times, I missed having someone to share my adventures with, I reminded myself of my courage to at least do it alone rather than miss experiencing it altogether by not doing it.

Socializing was and still is my middle name. I enjoy people and get out with friends or family frequently. I have met so many new friends as well. I was also lucky not to lose any of my friends after the divorce. By God's grace, the mutual friends who I shared with my ex remained my friends. Sadly, I can't say the same for him.

I also tried new things, one of which was golf. I suck, but I keep at it. In addition to my job, I began hospice volunteer work, which is extremely rewarding. Overcoming fears of trying something new really brought me back to the strong, driven, happy, and optimistic person that I used to be. Discovering who I was again and realizing the better version of myself that I was becoming was even more inspiring. I was actually beginning to create my own happiness.

It took me two years after my ex walked out to actually start dating again. Taking the time to grieve, cope and find myself were keys for me being ready to take the leap toward dating. It is important to take your time. It is daunting enough to muster up the courage to start dating again. You certainly don't want to fall into the trap of dating for the wrong reasons. Rediscover who you are. Be happy. You've got this!

Chapter 8: You Have to Kiss a Lot of Toads Before You Meet Your Prince

Vulnerable, scary as hell, nervous, excited, dread, and unconfident are just a few words to describe the many emotions you will experience when you think about dating. How long should I wait after my divorce before I start dating? How will I know I'm ready? How do I even go about dating again, especially in this new age of social media? How do I make this work with my kids? And oh, let's not forget sex. Someone is actually going to have to endure seeing me naked? I have to use condoms? I have to worry about STDs?

Profound Moment #12

Profound Moment #12 is that, don't overthink things ladies! Although these emotions and questions can be quite overwhelming, pull yourselves together. After all, you are not beginners. You know what you are doing. You've been "around the block" a time or two before and during your marriage. It's like riding a bike or driving a stick shift. Once you learn, you never forget, no matter how long it has been since you've done it. It's the same for dating and sex. I'm not going to lie. I talk a good game but that's because I've already done a bit of toad kissing since my divorce. Before any toads, I will admit, the emotions were real and I experienced all of them, but I am here to tell you that you will soon be saying, "Oh, that wasn't so difficult" "That wasn't as bad as I was expecting it to be," and "I can't believe I was so scared." My favorites are when you will say, "Wow that was fun and exhilarating!" and "My ex actually did me a favor!"

Wait Time

Professional opinions vary on this one but the general consensus seems to support waiting at least a year after your divorce is final, particularly if you're dating for a serious relationship. What is more important than the length of time is what you do during that time. It takes a year to get through significant events like the holidays, your birthday and doing things on your own. You need that time to cope, heal, and find yourself again. You need to figure out how to love yourself. How do you expect someone to love you if you don't love yourself? You need to be healthy in order to attract healthy people.

Your reasons for dating can also help determine how long you wait. If you want to date to avoid hurt, anger or loneliness, then you need to wait. These reasons will only set you up for failure. When you WANT to date instead of NEED to date, then you are ready. This becomes evident when the idea of going on a date comes into your mind and you don't want to immediately chase it out. In my case, I started dating two years after my ex walked out, a year after the divorce was final. Although I waited, I didn't start dating for a serious relationship. My ex was my one and only. I wanted to explore what was out there, figure out what I really wanted in a guy and, to be honest, find out what I was missing having only ever been with one man. AND BOY WAS I MISSING OUT ON A LOT!

Online Dating, Yay or Nay?

This is up for debate and purely a personal preference. For many of us when we were dating, there wasn't any Internet. Those who say Nay feel that searching for love online is desperate and/or scary. They are fearful of the process and the awkward or alarming situations that they may find themselves in meeting with strangers. They are more comfortable meeting someone by chance or through a blind date. Those who say Yay completely disagree. They feel that it is the best way to broaden your search and increase your odds of meeting someone compatible. These days there is a site for everyone. You just need to do your research on what each one has to offer and what you are looking for. There are even online resources available on how to get started and learn the basics of setting up profiles, taking them down, safety tips, etc. There are also scams that target online daters so educate yourself before venturing into this domain.

Personally, I'm a "Nay" for on-line dating. Call me old-fashioned, but I'm convinced that I'm going to happen upon my Mr. Right. I'm not having a problem meeting men and, initially, I was not ready for a serious relationship. Trust me, my friends occasionally pressured me to try online dating. They've even gone as far as to create fake profiles to show me what was out there. I love them dearly and get a kick out of their enthusiasm as they live vicariously through me but it just doesn't feel right. I'll never say never but right now… it's a no.

Most of the men I have met have been through friends. Some were blind dates and some I met at social events. I met a few of them at a bar, one at an NFL football game, and another one was my kitchen contractor. For me, I seem to be attracted to confident but not arrogant men, those with a sense of humor. Fun-loving and adventurous are also characteristics that I enjoy because I thrive on being social and trying new things. I rode on the back of a motorcycle, took a train ride, and experienced the exhilaration of a fast boat. I went on weekend trips to the mountains, to the woods, and to beaches. I like someone who is honest, attentive and enjoys intimacy. Quite frankly, good sex is high on my priority list.

Dating Tips

> 1. Face your fears. Take that leap. Remember, your apprehensions are normal. If the leap is too intimidating, take baby steps. Tell a few close friends that you are ready to meet people. Accept invitations to parties. Maybe even agree to a few blind dates. How you proceed will depend on what your intentions are for dating. Do you want a serious relationship? A short-term connection that might lead to something serious? Or just some fun for now? Be sure to convey these intentions as they might not be the same for your date. Transparency is important here.

2. Be optimistic. You attract what you put out into the universe. You will be tempted to make the mistake of negative thinking. "I can't believe I'm doing this." "This is awful." "How am I going to get through this?" Recognize these thoughts and let them go. Instead, see dating as an adventure, a learning opportunity, fun. Set reasonable expectations. No one is perfect and there will always be challenges. This is an experience for you to learn more about yourself and the new life you are creating.

3. Be confident. There's nothing wrong with you. Be honest about yourself, your past, your interests, and your kids. There is nothing wrong with being vulnerable. Don't be afraid to speak up about what you want and what you need, otherwise, you won't get it. You want someone who shares your values and likes you for you.

4. What you want matters. Know your priorities and values. You spent the better half of your life in a marriage where you sacrificed much of yourself for the needs of your husband and your children. Now it's your turn to put yourself first. It's not uncommon to date multiple men right out of the gate. I called this "my crazy phase," only to find out after some research, that it's not crazy at all. By dating several guys at a time, you avoid putting all your eggs in one basket and you are able to identify what you like and don't like moving forward in an actual serious relationship. Let's face it, after 15–20+ years of marriage, you already have a clear set of deal breakers. By dating multiple guys, you will discover some more! I like to call them my majors and minors. For me, the majors are absolute and relationship ending. These include lying, cheating, a small penis, unexciting sex, not a lover of family or someone who is not accepting of my children, just to name a few. For me, the minors, most of which seem silly, are not absolute relationship enders but could be if there is a significant additive effect. Some of these include snoring, ugly feet, and a hairy back. Again, no one is perfect but having been through what you have, don't you deserve to get as

much of what you want as possible? Just be sure that you clearly communicate that you are seeing others and for God Sake, practice safe sex!

5. Don't compare. Inevitably, you are tempted to compare your dates with your ex. You don't want someone who exhibits the behaviors of your ex that you didn't like. Learning and comparing are two completely different things. You learn from your ex to enhance your new relationships, not compare one to the other. Comparing does not allow faith in your present relationship and makes it harder to see your new partner at his fullest potential. Being hurt in your past relationship makes this faith difficult. Could this new guy hurt you? Sure, it's possible but he could also restore your faith in love. If you compare, you are focusing on the negative, the ways that things could go wrong and they will.

6. Slow and steady. You may want to start with texts and phone calls. Once you move on to dates, go on several. Dates should involve different activities. This will help you talk and get to know each other in different settings. Some dates should also involve your friends. It's nice to get their opinion and see how he interacts with them. This brings us to a very important point. Listen to the opinions of your friends and family. They are always looking out for your best interests. If there is a majority that expresses concern that something is wrong even when you think otherwise, listen, and be cautious. EVERYONE CAN'T BE WRONG!

7. There are some basic do's and don'ts when you are on a date. You should ask lots of questions but without it seeming as if you are interrogating the poor guy. Don't focus on your divorce or your ex and don't talk too much about your kids. Looking at your phone during the date is a definite "no no" unless to check for messages or calls from your kids. Watch how your date treats the waiter/waitress. A lot can be learned about a person, both good and bad, with these

observations. It's not a good idea to drink more than two drinks for reasons not requiring explanation and sex on the first date is not recommended but you probably will at some point go for it, just saying. Most of all, laugh and have fun!

8. If he says he wants or does not want something, believe him. Don't think you are going to change someone. So, you really like this guy and he says he wants the freedom to travel or go fishing when he wants. You need to decide if this is something you can live with or if it is a deal-breaker? You will not change him, so don't set yourself up for heartache or disappointment.

9. Give yourself a break. It's tough being out there dating again. Be patient with yourself and the process. Allow yourself to feel the emotions. Whether anxiety, guilt, or excitement, pay attention to your gut. It is usually always right. You deserve to be happy.

Don't Let Kids Stop You

As moms, the biggest fear is probably not wanting to upset our children or make them feel uncomfortable after all of the difficult transitions of the divorce. We don't want to disrupt the safe space of their home. It is important to respect them enough to be age-appropriately honest with them. Don't apologize for wanting to date but talk to them. Encourage them to ask questions and express their feelings and concerns. It's okay if they are sad or angry or nervous or judgmental. Make it clear that you will not be bringing men home and won't introduce them to anyone unless it becomes serious. The general rule of thumb is not to rush introducing a new partner to your family or your children, and to wait at least six months. In all honesty, most kids just want their parents to be happy. They are less likely to object to you dating than what you are imagining right now.

For me, with teenagers, I got the eye rolls and their comments of disgust, "I can't believe you get more action than me," "My friends think you're hot," "Going out for drinks again?" Let's be honest, it's hard enough for them to imagine me, their mother, with someone else, let alone imagine me having sex with a stranger. But that being said, they really do want me to be happy and have verbalized that on many occasions. My children have only met three of the men that I have dated, and these were men that I was able to see a forever with. Although it didn't wind up being my forever with any of them. The first relationship was at the two-year mark when my kids were 17, 15, and 13. They were still struggling with their father's relationship at that time, so they were definitely not super excited to have anyone in my life. The second relationship was when my kids were 23, 20, and 18 and he only met my son and youngest daughter as my oldest lives independently in another state. I actually introduced my kids to him after two months. By then, my children were well-adjusted with respect to their relationship with their father. They were super happy for me and really liked this guy. Unfortunately, a former girlfriend lured him back and that was the end of that. For the record, I refuse to compete for any man! And neither should you! At ages 24, 21 and 19, all of my children met the third guy that I was seriously dating. He was younger than me and my youngest was very judgmental at first. In time, they were all very supportive and glad to see me happy. Ultimately, this relationship ended as a result of dishonesty on his part, a definite deal-breaker for me.

Sex After Divorce

While much of this is very similar to the dating tips that we've already addressed, it is a step further than dating and does warrant sharing some additional information and cautions. After you have dealt with dating, the idea of sex can elicit those same feelings of anxiety. It is also possible that you are excited for it! Take it from me ladies, you will absolutely find that sex after divorce is way more fun and exhilarating than married sex!

I will admit, though, the first time is a little daunting and fraught with some confusing emotions. You might feel guilt, almost wondering if you are allowed to do this. There is always some apprehension. Will he be turned off by how my body looks? Will I do what he likes when we have sex? You will definitely have a "This is strange!" moment. But don't forget, this is someone new and there is an inherent excitement about that! Come on now. If I can do it after only having sex with one man my entire life, you can, too. Let go of the shame. It's okay to crave intimacy and sex. You know that you want to feel desired and sexy again! And you will! Let's face it, for most of you, your marriage was probably sexless or almost sexless toward the end. Remember, you are not a virgin. You are not inexperienced. I can assure you that you haven't forgotten how. You just need to get over the hump and when you do, you are going to be quite proud of the fact that you've still got it! Pretty soon, you will feel like you need to create a list of the guys so you can remember all of them. In case you are wondering, yes, I did create a list.

Trust me, you will be ecstatic to experience all the things you've been missing. For most of you, the first time back up on that bike will happen without any major incident, unlike myself. My first time, I just wanted to do it and get it over with. He was a very kind and respectful man. Very easy to talk to and open up to about my fears. I decided to have a few alcoholic beverages, you know, to relax me a bit, and diminish my inhibitions. I was actually feeling more confident. Well, then came the epic fail…intoxication. We were in the heat of the moment, just prior to the intercourse, and I felt sick. There I was naked on his bathroom floor with my head in the toilet. Now that's attractive… not! Bless him. He was so sweet and understanding. That being said, we did wind up having sex that night. I was determined and I persevered! I got over that hump! Hence, my list of men began.

I could write an entire book recounting some of my crazy and amusing escapades with the different men I have had sex with after my divorce, but I'm sure they would know who they were and I would be sued. I will say that each of them got a nickname. I started this because my friends lived vicariously through my sex tales, if nothing else, for a good laugh. I can tell some pretty funny stories. Like the time when I was visiting a girlfriend that lead to drinks on a boat, which lead to flirting with a gentleman on that boat, which would have led to sex if I hadn't been menstruating. I was just supposed to be visiting my girlfriend that evening so I was wearing a sanitary pad instead of a tampon. I mean nothing was going to happen visiting my girlfriend, right? Umm... wrong! Well there I was telling my friends the story of me in an unexpected and steamy make out session under the deck of this boat with a guy I had just met. Now, here is the funny thing. After a lot of hot and heavy kissing, he gets naked as do I except for my granny panties and my pad! Imagine having to explain that one in the heat of the moment. Still friends today, this guy and I continue to enjoy a good laugh about that night. Even though we didn't have sex, he was branded "Naked Man." Sorry, I digressed. So, my friends could never remember these guys by name when I would recount my sexual encounters, but they were able to keep up and keep track of them by their nicknames. This was because their nicknames were based, in some way, on my experience with each of them. In good company with Naked Man was Stage 5 Clinger, Hotel Hook-Up, Uranus, The Butler, The Stalker, Twenty-five, and Thirty-four just to name a few. It got to a point where my friends wanted input on naming the guys. Based on the nicknames, you can only imagine the stories.

Although a great chapter title, in all seriousness, none of these men were toads; they just weren't right for me or I wasn't right for them. With some, there was no chemistry. Some were too arrogant. Some were dishonest. And quite frankly, some were just not good in bed. My advice, as with dating, is not to rush and/or have sex out of revenge. Heal, find yourself, and get used to overcoming some of your anxieties by dating. You need to realize that your first sexual experience after your divorce is usually transitional and he will, most likely, not be a keeper. Allow yourself to meet and have sex with other guys. Enjoy the fact that sex is no longer like the boring sex that you had when you were married. There are no rules here and you now have choices. In spite of what you may think, there is quite a variety out there. Different types of men bring different types of sexual experiences and a new bag of tricks to the bedroom, of sorts. Not to disappoint you, ladies, but from nursing for all these years and from my actual experiences with men, there is no way of guessing a man's penis size. My expectations have been wrong so many times. I have been both pleasantly surprised and not so pleasantly surprised on many occasions. Performance can also be unpredictable. Don't judge a book by its cover. If I think a guy has potential but the sex was not so great, I usually give it another try just to be sure. After all, he could have had performance anxiety. I'm definitely a second chance kind of gal. Let's face it, I'm far from perfect. There is so much to gain, and self-knowledge is no exception. You will grow and learn more about yourself and what you need or want with each partner. Give yourself that opportunity. Don't settle or set your standards too low to avoid being alone.

Having mentioned younger men, I'm going to veer slightly off course for a bit since I have a bit of experience here and feel it necessary to impart some insight. If sex with a younger man happens for you, you will undoubtedly find this super exciting as you are struggling to find your sexual self again. It's flattering. Hell, the fact that someone young finds you attractive and still wants to have sex with you after seeing you naked is empowering in itself! When it comes to sex, he's the gift that keeps on giving with little to no downtime. If you have the opportunity and it's your thing, I say go for it, ladies, as long as he is respectful and not using you for a meal ticket. Just be realistic. Understand that you have life experience and wisdom. As much as he or you might think he is mature for his age or an old soul, he's still young. Wisdom comes with age. Obviously, my ability to trust took a big hit when I was abandoned. Maybe I was protecting my heart by listening to my head. And just when I say don't overthink it, there I was overthinking it. The way I saw it, I was the only one to get hurt. Even if it lasted, when he reached 45, the age when my husband left me for another woman, I would be 68. Surely my looks, my sex drive, and my body's ability to respond to intercourse will be very different than what it is now. He would want excitement and leave me to find it. This can be quite a dilemma. Let's be clear, I'm not at all advising against having sex with a younger man. By all means, go for it! I'm here to tell you that it's awesome! I'm also not advising against a serious relationship with a younger man. You just need to tread cautiously and be realistic about your intentions and verbalize them with your younger partner as he should verbalize his intentions to you. Again, don't overthink it. There's no way to predict the future. He very well could be your forever person. Don't set yourself up for failure by being negative.

This leads directly into your need to be honest with yourself about your reasons for having sex. These are the same as your reasons for dating and we've already identified revenge and not wanting to be alone as absolute "no no's." Are you just in it for casual sex or are you looking for something long term? Brief flings are an ego boost and broaden your horizons. There is no doubt that trust and opening your heart again are some big obstacles to maneuver. Are you really ready to get emotionally attached? Unfortunately, as women, our biology makes it hard to just have sex but it can be done. We have sex, which leads to orgasms, which lead to our brains being inundated with oxytocin. This hormone stimulates feelings of attachment. Don't confuse intimacy with love. If casual or "friends with benefits" is what you want in order to experience the variety, it may be helpful to have sex with guys that you have a connection with but don't see a future with. If it's your thing, maybe having what I call a rotation of men will work for you to limit attachments.

Initially, for me, it was mainly casual sex. It was definitely about figuring out what I was missing. I felt like a teenager again, anticipatory butterflies in my stomach and make-out sessions. For the sake of defending my honor, I wasn't "easy" nor did I sleep with every guy I met. I was very selective when it came to sexual partners. I enjoyed having no strings attached, trying new things, fantasy fulfillment, and becoming comfortable telling men what I wanted. It was definitely a time to try the sexual things that my ex would laugh at me for trying when we were married. As a result of sex after divorce, I discovered new sex toys, on-line porn, and the sexual behaviors that I enjoy and don't enjoy. Don't knock it till you try it when it comes to masturbation, anal sex, role play, sex swings, or being tied up and blind-folded, just saying. Although rare as a woman, I was the sexually deprived partner in my marriage. I would never have ended my marriage because of it, but once the decision was made for me, I came to realize that a healthy sexual relationship is a priority for me for any future, long-term relationship. I have sex fairly early on with my partners because I don't want to develop feelings or get attached if the sex is not good. Not an issue for everyone and not everyone's cup of tea, just another reason to be aware of.

Having laid all this out, it wouldn't be wise if I didn't endorse responsibility and safety. Be smart. You know what's out there and what can happen. Practice safe sex. You don't want to get pregnant or acquire any STDs. He might say he has had a vasectomy or his penis may look clean, but it doesn't mean that it is true. Use a CONDOM until you know otherwise! Just like dating, be cautious. The fact that men lie about not being married or being sexually involved with other women is more common than you think. Make sure friends or family know where you are and don't take men home. The evening news is never short on the whack jobs and stalkers that are out there. Don't forget, you have your children to protect as well.

Inevitably, as you date and have sex, you will find that you really like one or two or three of them but they just want to be friends. You might even be shocked to find that they are married or have a girlfriend and you wouldn't dare go there after what you've been through. After all, truly moral women would never hurt another woman in such a vile way. You will reach a time when you want to move from casual dating and sex to a long-term relationship and this doesn't have to be marriage. To each, their own.

Although I have not yet found my prince, I have not given up on kissing frogs. I have faith that the man for me is out there. I'm actually enjoying this phase of exploration and transformation in my life. Don't be afraid of this part of your journey! If nothing else, while you wait for Prince Charming, experiment and, at least, find the right sexual partner for your needs or at least for a night or two. **You've got this, ladies!**

Chapter 9: What Doesn't Kill You Makes You Stronger

"Stand up straight and realize who you are, that you tower over your circumstances. You are a child of God. Stand up straight."

Maya Angelou

Wow! That is certainly powerful! She also says, "We may encounter many defeats but we must not be defeated."

Profound Moment #13

Well ladies, it's time for **Profound Moment #13**, embrace your future! You have been empowering yourself as you have read each chapter of this book, arming yourself with knowledge. Now it's time to act. It's quite an adventure, for sure, but you are ready.

You are in charge of your new destiny. You need to recognize where you are in your journey and start from there. Are you just finding out that your husband is leaving? Or are you drowning in the overwhelming emotions? Are you embroiled in a bitter court battle? Or are you struggling with anger and bitterness? Are you wrestling with parenting? Or are you at the phase of dating and having sex? It doesn't matter where you are or the mistakes you have made along the way; positive action is a necessity. Confucius said it best, "It does not matter how slowly you go as long as you do not stop." You are already aware of the many challenges you have faced or still have to face. It feels like hell, but you have to keep going. Don't let fear keep you from being happy. You, and only you are responsible for your own happiness, no one else.

Take Control

If you haven't already, start by taking control of some of the simple aspects of your life. Create YOUR HOME. No matter where you land and consider home after your divorce, make it your own. Whether it's buying a new bed and bed linens, painting, or in my case, a new kitchen, being in charge of your own space is empowering.

Who you surround yourself with will also have an impact on your future. I'm sure you can easily identify those people in your life who you can trust and rely on. These are your keepers. Offload those who don't make you feel good or who are not healthy for you. You need to move up, not down, forward not back. Take choosing YOUR PEOPLE seriously.

Evaluate your job situation. Are you happy with what you do? If the answer is yes, then set your sights on the next step. If your answer is no, change is in your control. Grant it, a job or career change is significant and stressful, but finding your place is revitalizing and, again, empowering.

It is also important to take charge of your money. You need to educate yourself financially. You need to be able to understand how to budget, to invest money, and to plan for retirement. Learn how to save money in taxes. If possible, get a good financial advisor and/or tax accountant. This is a good start to embracing your future.

Continue to Cope

Life will continue to throw you an occasional curveball. You will continue to struggle emotionally, at times. Breathe. Let me say that again… Breathe. You now have knowledge and knowledge is power. You might find that you reread this book at different times during your life journey or you might just re-visit certain chapters. For that matter, the internet is a brilliant source. Search engines are your friend, so use them. There is a wealth of information out there. It is healthy to search for reminders or new ways to navigate your transitions. Those coping strategies that I still find helpful, even years later, include: spending time with family and friends, yoga, meditation, my music playlists, traveling, prayer, my grateful journal and movies. Don't judge, but there are times when I am obsessed with Hallmark movies. Nothing like a good, "happy tears" moment to maintain your faith in romance and love. These coping tools have become part of my days, and others are reserved for my more trying times. You do you. Find what works and incorporate it into your life. Taking care of yourself will allow everything else to fall into place.

Be Positive and Inspire

As I've said before, the universe is like a magnet. You attract what you put out there. Have you ever known someone who has a "woe is me" personality, an Eeyore of sorts from Winnie the Pooh? It's almost crazy how they have a consistent black cloud that follows them. You find it almost unbelievable that they find themselves in so many bad circumstances. Well, it's not crazy. The more negative you are, the more negative that will come your way. You need to shift this way of thinking. It's "I can do it," not "I can't do it;" "This is going to be great," not "This is going to suck." Until you change to a more positive perspective, you will not attract what you want.

Try creating a vision board. You may even want to create more than one throughout your journey. Attach to your board, everything you desire in your life… your hopes, your dreams. It can include magazine pictures, words, photos, or objects. Place it where you can see it every day. Give yourself some time to concentrate on it, reaffirm your intentions, and believe it. It will release you from your limiting thoughts and allow you to know that the possibilities are really unlimited. What a positive way to start your day! You will soon find that things you want will come to you. Mark my word, you will be astounded!

I even went as far as to put a picture of a car that I really wanted as my desktop wallpaper. I saw it every time I opened my laptop. Can you believe I had that car almost two years later and I wasn't actively searching for it?! It was nothing short of incredible! I created a new vision board, a little over a year ago, that includes inspirational messages. It has pictures of open hearts to encourage me to keep my heart open no matter how many times it gets hurt. It has pictures of full hearts, handsome men, glasses, and magnifiers to illustrate my readiness for love and my desire for the ability to see and recognize it. It includes the number of my desired weight. And lastly, I have publishing pictures on it. Can you believe it? One year and I'm actually doing it!

It could seem unusual, but now more than ever, you are in a position to be a positive role model who inspires others, especially if you have children. You have experienced unimaginable heartbreak. Your life has been turned upside down. How you respond will be critical. What do you wish to portray to the outside world, your family, your friends, and your kids? Everyone will be watching, particularly your children. They are always watching and learning. Show them your strength and perseverance as you move forward with clarity, confidence, positivity, and hope. Family and friends will be inspired by the person you become. Use your life experience to pay it forward by being there for someone else going through a divorce.

Motivate yourself. Figure out how to change that light switch or light fixture and how to change that tractor or jet ski battery. Get on that tractor and cut your grass. Assemble that shelving unit. Watch online videos to figure out how to troubleshoot things. It's extremely empowering! It's not only badass, but it's sexy! You can do anything you put your mind to. If you want flowers, don't hope someone will buy them for you, buy them for yourself. Pray and express gratitude, if it's your thing. They will do wonders for inspiring your soul.

"What Doesn't Kill You Makes You Stronger," they say. And it's the truth! These words and Kelly Clarkson's song, Stronger, have been my mantra since day one. The lyrics of the song are honest, inspirational, and poignant. "In the end, the day you left was just my beginning." Hell yes! Amen, sister! Remember, you are beautiful and you are strong. Take charge of your new beginning. No one else can do it for you. The future is exciting and bright.

You've got this Ladies! Pull from your faith and your strength. **You've got this!!!**

Chapter 10: Life Is Good

After eight years, I have been able to create a very fulfilling and happy life. There were many highs and lows and many struggles and triumphs. I have not only reached the light at the end of the tunnel but I have endured and overcome. I have successfully crossed that bridge and life is good!

In terms of my children, we have made it through drivers' licenses, college visits, proms, high-school graduations, summer jobs, and college graduations. My youngest entered college a year ago, and if all goes well, will be the next nurse in the family in three years. You have no idea how much this warms my heart. My oldest just graduated summa cum laude and is currently embarking on her amazing, "big girl," dream job. The pride I feel still brings happy tears to my eyes. My middle child will graduate next year with honors and assures me that he will do amazing things. He might not believe me, but I have faith in him for sure. I couldn't be more grateful that they have become the responsible, respectful, kind, trusting, and successful humans I was praying for throughout this endeavor as a single parent.

What's even more extraordinary is that my children are so proud of me. They like the person I have become and they tell me that often. They can't believe how relaxed and easy-going I am now. As adults, they can, now, truly understand what I have been through and how far I've come. When your kids tell you that they admire you and that you are their role model, there is nothing more endearing and uplifting. They appreciate me and I certainly appreciate them. Now that they are grown, it's fun to switch gears and be their friend since they no longer need me as much as a parent. The circle of life and the resilience of the human spirit are awe-inspiring.

I still have all of my fantastic family! I get a call, just about every day from my mom to check up on me and to chat. I'm an open book so she always gets the play by play of what has transpired since our previous conversation. She puts me on speaker so my dad can listen and participate. I'm so proud of how far they have come in learning the functions of a smartphone since it took my siblings and I quite a few years to convince them to transition from their flip phones. I am very close with my sister and brother, and family gatherings are always a hoot as we cut each other off and talk above each other. It's not survival of the fittest but survival of the loudest in my family. Whether it's around the kitchen table at our parents' house or around our favorite corner table at their local bar, the conversation is guaranteed to get loud and many times foul and always ends in tears of laughter. I am so blessed to have them, their significant others, and their children in my life. My heart is full of gratitude for them.

All my friends are still in my life as well. They have been my lifeline throughout this crazy journey of mine. Whether it's dinner, drinks, boating, or vacationing, these connections will be forever. The memories we have created and continue to create make me smile inside and out. My seven closest girlfriends who have always been there for me as well as my sister and sister-in-law accompanied me on a catamaran sailing adventure throughout the British Virgin Islands for my 50th birthday, three years ago. The laughter was plenty, and the memories will be lifelong. There was a detainment at customs, skinny dipping in our underwear, silly photoshoots in the sand, snorkeling for conch, endless cocktails, late night cabin giggle sessions, pole dancing onboard, Mary Poppins who had everything we needed, a birthday serenade by a boat full of men, pin the dick on the man, and I'm pretty sure I broke my finger before we even set sail. I was so grateful for all of them being so willing to share my special day that I planned an Oscars Night. The crew of three were exceptional. They made an incredible meal and laid out a plastic red carpet. I had a speech for each person with an accompanying small plastic Oscar statue engraved with an award title that was individual to each one of them. They included an Outstanding Female Performance in a Weekly Wine Night Role, a Loyal Friend Role, a Daily Phone Call Role, a Dynamic Duo Role, a Voice of Reason Role, a Dealing with Drama Role, a Supporting Sister Role, and a Sympathetic Sister Role. It was so important for me to convey to each of them how important they were to my healing. What a memorable night and phenomenal birthday vacation. It was the perfect way to celebrate a milestone birthday—my 50th. Gratitude is still a very big part of my life, and I pay it forward in any way that I can.

Now that my children are off in other states, there is quite a bit more "me" time. Life has brought with it many shifts in focus, from school, to my work, to my husband and children and now back to my work and me. I'm still very invested in my profession as a critical care transport nurse. Incredibly, I continue to love my job. I have had the pleasure of working with extremely competent and entertaining staff members over the years. I am now able to return to 12-hour night shifts, which I prefer, and I have been able to work more hours now that the kids are gone. It's so nice to arrive at work and everyone is grateful that I am there. We are responsible for transporting some extremely sick patients who require state of the art equipment to keep them alive from one hospital to the next. We've been through the unknowns of SARS, H1N1 and COVID-19. This job can be both physically and emotionally demanding much of the time. There was a time when I started this job that I was one of the youngest in the department. Now I am one of the oldest, so, to still be appreciated by my co-workers when I come to work is as reassuring as it is gratifying.

Emotionally, I am doing extremely well. There are rare twinges of resentment surrounding certain memories that pop up or if I happen to see my ex and the girlfriend but it is very brief and short lived. My ex still remains in the same relationship. My kids are still not accepting of it, and each deals with it in different ways that work for them. I have always encouraged a relationship with their father even in the most difficult of times. Although he stumbled greatly as a father after he left, he has put forth the effort to create stronger bonds to the extent that he is capable of. I am grateful because they love their dad and make it a point to spend time with him when they are in town. It definitely makes my heart happy.

I am now able to share with the kids many joyful memories of their dad and I when we were together. Many times, the kids will talk with me about their own relationship issues and I will share how their father and I dealt with similar situations. Many times, it leads to stories that are either heartwarming, funny, or both. I'm not sure how it came about but I was just telling my youngest daughter the other day about a moment on our wedding day that was so small but so epic in what it meant to me that I will never forget it. I got to the altar and my hands were shaking with nerves when my father put my hands into the hands of her father's. I told her how at that moment, he saw them shaking, grabbed them both into his so firmly and his eyes just said, "it's ok, I've got you." It was probably one of the most tender and touching moments of my life. It's so nice to be able to share memories such as these. It's important for our children to know that there was great love and that they came from great love. I want them to have faith that when they get married, their relationships will last. I want them to believe in the "for better or worse" and that relationships take work. I don't want them to be afraid of a "one and only" relationship turning into a marriage. I have no regrets for marrying my one and only. I've shared with my kids our trips to Costa Rica and Alaska before we were married and our trips to Hawaii on our honeymoon and our 10th anniversary. I would tell them how we would rent fleabag motel rooms just to be able to spend time at the beach when we had very little money. Luckily for our children, I was able to take them to some of the same Hawaiian Islands their father and I visited, and their father has taken them to Costa Rica.

Now, quite a bit of our conversations surround their careers and I am able to share how we made our way in the beginning and how hard work and teamwork resulted in my successful career and their father's successful business. It is important for them to know that we were happy and that they were a big part of that happiness. Their father recently got a new boat that was previously owned, and my youngest shared that he spends a lot of time working on it. The former me might have been snarky about it but the new and improved me expressed to her that I was happy for him. I told her that captaining an offshore fishing boat was always his dream, and that I was sure he was enjoying tinkering with it and making it his own. But just so you know that I'm not perfect, when she shared that he ran it aground on his journey from South Carolina to Maryland and how much it cost to fix it, I was smiling inside and did gloat a bit to several of my friends. I know, I know, bad karma is coming for me for sure. But let's face it, sometimes you just need a smiling moment to offset the twinge of bitterness. No one is perfect, right?

Unfortunately, due to the ugliness of our journey after he left, my ex and I do not speak. There is no communication of any kind. What does need to be communicated goes through the children. Surprisingly, it seems to work. The kids have adapted to the fact that there is much more peace in their lives as a result. It's kind of ironic that for a few years now, I've been willing to change that. Although I would never forgive his significant other for what she did to our family, I am now able to look past the indiscretions of my ex for the sake of our children. Unfortunately, there has been no progress on the communication front because the children have conveyed his hatred for me. It still astounds me as to how he can walk out of his life to supposedly be happier in another and he hates me. The higher road continues to be a mainstay in my world and doing what's best for my children will always be my priority. Life will never be perfect, and I am okay with that. You just need to do what you can to turn those lemons into the best lemonade you possibly can.

I still own and live in the home that our children grew up in as well as the beach house where they have created great memories. Both are still very important to them so I have made no decisions to downsize at this point in my life. My D-I-Y list of accomplishments continues to grow as renovation and maintenance are just about a full-time job, but I make it all work somehow. You should see me out there on the zero-turn tractor mowing the lawn. I'm a badass.

Life is so busy that I have not struggled with having an empty nest. When I'm not working or maintaining homes, I'm fishing, spending time at the beach, boating, and traveling. I love crabbing and rock fishing in the Chesapeake Bay, flounder fishing in the back bays at the beach, and offshore fishing in the Atlantic Ocean for tuna, mahi and white marlin. I just recently had the thrill of catching a tile fish which was reeled in from 800 ft. on an electronic reel! My dad had a love of fishing as does my ex-husband. Again, lots of great memories, and now I have new ones on my own. Maybe it's my Aries fire sign, but traveling and adventure are necessities for me. I enjoy the anticipation and excitement that exploration brings. Now that my children are all in different states, I have new places to visit. I am on-again off-again with golfing. I just need more hours in the day. I have recently become scuba certified and plan to embark on a new set of underwater adventures. This was intimidating at first and is still a bit scary when I consider what can go wrong but ultimately, it has probably been the most exhilarating thing I have ever done. Let's see if this holds true after I jump out of an airplane and parachute to the earth. That's going to be on my next vision board!

In terms of love, Mr. Right is out there. We just haven't found each other yet. My life is full and happy, and I refuse to settle. If I'm being completely honest, I've had a great deal of fun dating and even more fun having sex. I've actually gotten pretty damn good at it! As a result, I have learned so much about myself but I am definitely ready for a forever relationship. I have had my heart broken three times since my divorce which, I will admit, takes me back a couple steps for a bit, but I will never give up on love. It's part of who I am. I am meant to share my life with someone. I am the forever optimist. As I've stated before, we are responsible for our own happiness and no one else can provide that for us.

I am determined to be a positive role model in all aspects of my life. I'm not perfect by any means, and I still stumble. I just hope that sharing my story and the lessons that I've learned can help you in your journey to a peaceful and fulfilling life of purpose and happiness. With all of the goodness that has been bestowed upon me along the way, I try to pay it forward in any way that I can. As women, we have great strength and perseverance, much more than we ever thought possible. Life is good. I wish you well! I wish you abundance in all things! And I wish you empowerment! **You've got this, ladies!**

Acknowledgements

I am so blessed that God has put so many amazing people in my path at exactly the right times during my journey.

To Wendy Anderson, my voice of reason. There are not enough words to express the impact of your empathetic ear and your many words of wisdom. Thank you for having the courage to relive your nightmare in order to help me through mine.

To Darlene Hackett, my friend who always includes me. Your kindness and friendship have played a major part in me living again. And to her husband, Bill, thanks for putting up with your work wife.

A big shout out to the rest of my Girl Gang: Lisa Hager, Deb Brazell, Beth Bazell, and Sharon Slotterback. Thanks for being my village. Never a dull moment for sure. Because of all of you, I will never be lonely or without laughter.

For my counselor, Julie Dixon, you were a blessing to our family. Your professionalism, empathy, and kindness were invaluable for keeping me sane during some unbelievably dark times. Thank you for helping me to see the light at the end of the tunnel and to move forward in amazingly positive ways.

I am forever grateful for my incredible lawyer, Sam Brown. You showed me nothing but kindness and compassion. Your words of wisdom offered through your own life's journey still resonate with me today. Thank you for taking a broken woman and turning her into a formidable warrior.

For my financial advisor, Jamie Kujawski, I will always be confused and you will always try to clarify with examples. Thank you for your patience on my journey to financial independence. Your friendship and your willingness to share your story were definitely a great source of encouragement. Cheers to shots and a rhyme!

My best friend, Joan Martin, thank you for always showing up. Your loyalty to our friendship warms my heart. I am so grateful that you and yours will forever be part of my family.

My co-worker and friend, Lynnette Barker, I will never forget your support during those first days, weeks and months. I'm not sure how I could have made it through shifts without you. Your social media posts still provide me with some timely, smiling moments. Thank you!

And finally, to my wonderful family, thank you for always listening to my play by play. I am grateful for our love, our fun and our TMI, all of which have been a great support over these last eight years. Mom, Dad, Debbie, Pee Wee, Tom, Daniela, Tim, Ryan, and Nathan, I love you all!

And most of all to my babies, Emily Elizabeth, David Lee, and Anna Margaret, you had to endure some pretty crazy circumstances as a result of the divorce and you have emerged as caring, respectful and responsible human beings. Your resilience and successes make me so proud! You continue to love and trust and for that, I am grateful.

To my coaching team at Sai.coach, I cannot thank you enough for helping me navigate the publishing process. The resources your team provided met my every expectation and then some. You all are the best!

www.ingramcontent.com/pod-product-compliance
Lightning Source LLC
Chambersburg PA
CBHW021344090426
42742CB00008B/736